Editorial

CHARLES BOYLE

"By way of" – that's a fine opening gambit (see page 106), and I've cribbed it for here. I'd asked Ian Duhig for a piece on Leeds, thinking I'd get something on how, in a city more compact but no less various than London, poets of different stripes can't help but rub up against each other. He delivered on that, but the bonus extra was even more to my liking: a celebration of reading as "travelling without landmarks".

Reading – listening, attending, being thrilled or begging to differ and sometimes both – is primary. Writing may follow; it's not compulsory. Further down the line, editing, even (and I'll slot in here a sincere thankyou to the Poetry Society for inviting me to guest-edit this issue, for trusting me to a degree I don't myself, and to the many, many people who sent in their work). Reading is possibly the most demanding, pointless, pleasurable, exploratory, active thing we can do. We read, take a hint, follow a hunch and read something else. If we get lost, so much the better. If we pause to look back, we may well find that we've crossed a border or two without even noticing that they were there.

"Border", here, is a metaphor. As is "travelling", as is "landmarks". It seems we need them. But I think that writers (journalists especially) need the border one more than readers: a new generation defines itself *against* an older one, and one company of writers pitches its own potential *against* the perceived limitations of another one. As a reader, without a stake in these disputes, I've always found that a liking for chalk doesn't disqualify me from also liking cheese. Not all chalk, not all cheese, but I take my pleasures from where I will, and no one generation or band of poets has a monopoly on these. Nor, of course, does any single art form, which is why you'll find notice taken here of cross-overs between poetry and fine art, prose fiction, song-writing and the stage. Poetry cannot, for its own health, stay at home all day.

I've juggled a little with the structure of the magazine – the poems are presented here in two separate runs, and the reviews and essays likewise – but space has been a problem. A small experiment occurs on page 128, where I asked David Morley if he might adapt his online Twitter reviews to cover a large number of pamphlets in a limited space; think of this as the reviewing equivalent of speed-dating. The hope is simply this: that readers may be prompted to inquire further, to nose around, to wander off at a tangent, *by way of* what they find here.

LIVE POETRY
AT SOUTHBANK CENTRE
AUTUMN 2012

THURSDAY 4 OCTOBER
National Poetry Day Live

Join Southbank Centre and the Poetry Society for this celebration of poetry featuring Dannie Abse, Helen Mort and many others. Drop into one of the tents inspired by Deborah Warner's commission for London 2012 Festival, Artichoke's Peace Camp.

**The Clore Ballroom at Royal Festival Hall, 1pm – 6pm
Free**

THURSDAY 25 OCTOBER
Sharon Olds

Sharon Olds is one of America's great poets and a powerful reader of her work. Join us to celebrate the publication of her twelfth collection *Stag's Leap*.

**Purcell Room at Queen Elizabeth Hall, 7.45pm
£10**

WEDNESDAY 7 NOVEMBER
Chris McCabe, Julia Copus and Jacob Polley

Hear three poets reading from their diverse new collections.

**Level Five Function Room at Royal Festival Hall, 6.30pr
£8**

THURSDAY 29 NOVEMBER
Saul Williams' Literary Mix Tape

Acclaimed poet and musician Saul Williams is back, following his sold out show at this summer's London Literature Festival. He share the stage with some of his favourite poets and spoken word artists.

**Queen Elizabeth Hall, 7.45pm
£15, £12**

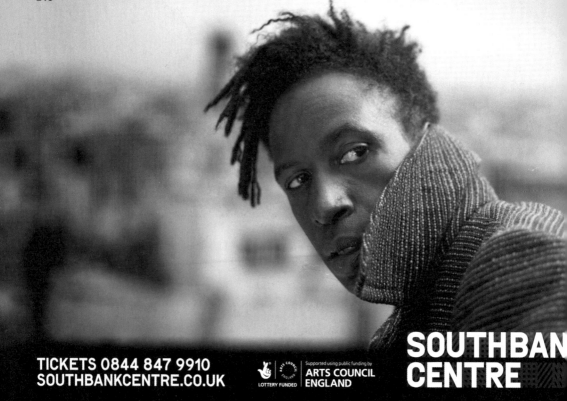

**TICKETS 0844 847 9910
SOUTHBANKCENTRE.CO.UK**

LOTTERY FUNDED   Supported using public funding by ARTS COUNCIL ENGLAND

**SOUTHBAN
CENTRE**

Contents

Volume 102:3 Autumn 2012

POETRY SOCIETY ANNUAL LECTURE

POEMS

ESSAYS & REVIEWS

Pages from Tom Phillips's A Humument *are reproduced in black-and-white on pages 5, 34 and 83. © The artist, 2012.*

her in a way in which a woman could not have described
them if they had not been part of
her own actual life; and yet, on the other hand, I constantly
said also, would a woman, if they had been, have had the
courage to describe them? There is another supposition
which once or twice occurred to me, and that is that though
her whole story be true, it is the story not of the authoress
but of some other woman, who had revealed it to her. I
thought, you see, that though she might have shrunk from
describing herself, she might yet have had nerve enough for
a _post-mortem_ examination of a sister."

"Your supposition is wrong," said Countess Z—— quietly.
"It is her own story. She has changed, as you have observed,
the names of places and people; and also a number of other
accidental circumstances; but so far as essentials are con-
cerned, she has, to the best of my belief, not written a word
that is not absolutely true. In this volume you have her
life, and the life of another, turned literally inside out."

"And do you mean to tell me," I exclaimed, "that a
woman of position and reputation, a woman too so sensitive
as she must have been and in some ways so extraordinarily
innocent, really proposed to publish such a confession about
herself, with such a mere pretence of a veil thrown over her
own identity? There are things in that Journal which the
most callous woman would hide."

"There is nothing in that Journal," said Countess Z——,
"which a callous woman could feel; and it is the sensitive
women, and not the callous ones, for whom confession is
sometimes a necessity. The veil, however, which you think
so transparent, would really have been thick enough for
every practical purpose. The hidden drama of which you
have just seen the opening, was unsuspected by any one during
the life-time of the two chief actors; it is not likely to be
suspected now that they are both dead. The very people
who knew them whilst it was in progress, and indeed took
unconscious parts in it, would never make any account of it,
be likely to connect it with them, unless names and localities
were mentioned by their actual names; so the changes made
by the authoress, slight as you may think them, would have
been more than sufficient, supposing her book had been
published, to have preserved her secret from even her own
acquaintances. And now," Countess Z—— continued, "I will

Dan O'Brien

The War Reporter Paul Watson
and Dirty Business

On foot, Somalia and Afghanistan
are the same. Combat boots sink ankle-deep
in the bone-gray talc, bursts of jetting earth
coating teeth and lenses. The peacekeepers
in Belet Huen baited petty thieves with
food and water. Shot a man in the back
as he ran. Could not lift his black body
without it flopping to pieces. A boy
found hiding in a toilet. Some soldiers
waterboarded him, then sodomized him
with a broomstick. Extinguished cigarettes
on his penis. Then beat him with meal packs
till he died. At a miserable crossroads
years later, things are done neatly. When roads
leap out in shrapnel and claim another
soldier for death, a bulldozer disrobes
the walls of a Pashtun village. Money
changes hands, teenagers handed over
to police for torture. Even children
race from the peacekeepers as they approach
on foot. White faces under blue helmets
tell me: It's dirty business, but then war
always is.

The Poet Runs

from LA at sunset. Women's faces
are slick masks thanks to Botox. Some men look
embalmed and tan also. Helicopters
over Brentwood like they're still following
OJ's white Bronco. While I'm soldiering
up Amalfi to Sunset the Palisades
look more like the hills of South Korea
on *MASH*. Or Tuscany. While you're somewhere
in Kandahar. I've filled my prescription
for Zoloft, Paul. I'm enjoying living
in my strange new home. Along the margin
of the sea upsetting a conspiracy
of gulls into whole shoals lifting. Hot girls
watching the sun set. *Who is that running*
with me? this shadow, over my shoulder
in the sun and sand. Like my brother or
some other fallen angel. Shackleton
staggering through the blizzard with his men
starving, delirious. How they kept seeing
a fourth with them. How they kept asking, *Who*
is that fourth who walks always beside you?
and Eliot stole that for his *Waste Land* but
revised four into three for poetic
reasons. On the horizon sand plovers
bundling like a haze of corpseflies before
the satiate smudge of fire. The rolling foam
of breaking waves is suddenly sublime
ice floes. Is the man running after me
the man who haunts you? And what could he want
from me?

John Gohorry
from The Age of Saturn

From Don Francisco José de Goya y Lucientes to Frederico Giovanni Scardanelli, dated March 1823

Your letter, Esteemed Sir, reaches me in difficult times.
Everywhere, factions contend, brigades of one colour
marching to dispossess those of another of what all

hold precious as birthright, aristocracies threatened
by mutinous soldiers, and poor people everywhere
in despair at the price of bread. Uprisings break out,

are suppressed, and erupt in the next town; militias
assemble, demonstrate, and dissolve. From streets
corpses are hurried to hastily dug graves and buried

under cover of darkness with no military honours,
and every day from riverbanks where processions
once took their breast-beating paths to shrines rise

lamentations of widows and orphans. In such times
is it possible not to ask 'What makes us people we are?'
And for how long can one say 'This is the person I am'?

Seeing, one says, is believing, but I have been working
on two studies where what is not seen teases the mind
with thoughts to be guessed at. In a dimly lit room

somewhere indefinite, Gonzalez pleasures himself;
his eyes gleam and his tongue is a bell-clapper to which
all the women of Spain give attention. Two watch

the cradle and jerk of imagined hands in his trousers;
the older, herself long since a traveller in this country,
smiles broadly in pleasure or envy, the younger looks on

It is a few weeks before the French invasion of Spain on 17 April, with the intention of restoring the rule of Ferdinand VII, who for the past three years has been a prisoner of the Cortes in Cadiz. The invasion culminated in the Battle of Trocadero (31 August) where Ferdinand was freed and restored to (absolute) power.

Goya's Two Women and a M

with the cautious, discreet eyes of someone watching
a small bird splash in a pond. What arouses Gonzalez?
Some inner upconjured vision of lace, doeskin, velvet,

a flicker of hair in the firelight. Yet I acknowledge him
as my blood brother of visions. From the tip of a brush
I flood pigment over the plaster, the sweep of my arm,

wrist, fingers spreading stain everywhere, what I see
spilled onto the walls while witnesses afterwards meet
to disparage a sterile act carried out in a hermitage

as the state's falling in ruins. Elsewhere, I have painted
a Judith, sword raised in the halflight of Holofernes' tent,
on the verge of despatching the tyrant. Her maidservant

*Judith and Holofernes.
No Judith emerged in
Spain to assassinate
Ferdinand VII, who,
after Trocadero,
despite promising
amnesty, took
bloodthirsty revenge
on those who had
opposed him.*

has her hands clasped in prayer, and when the blade falls
those prayers will be answered. I have shown neither
the general, drunk on his bed, nor her triumphant hand

holding his head aloft while the grisly torso spurts blood,
one being the antecedent, and the other the consequent
of this moment where courage converted intention

to action, and so delivered Israel. Fires burn in the streets,
mobs march, and the Assyrian everywhere carries out
acts of repression and bloodshed. What Israel needs

is a young widow of moderate beauty, strongly resolved,
with a blade in the folds of her skirt. While Everyman
flees for his life from the armies, or in some private room

imagines her being unveiled as the silk wraps slip away
till she lies naked and yielding, she asks her servant to pray
and, bravely drawing her knife, goes for the jugular.

The poem is taken from sequence of thirty-four verse letters supposedly exchanged between Goya and Hölderlin between 1819 and 1828. For Hölderlin 'The Age of Saturn' represented a vanished idyll, when the earth yielded up its harvest without need of human labour, and when there were no troublesome distinctions between good and bad, right and wrong. Goya was drawn to the way Saturn responded to the prophecy that one of his children would overthrow him and, troubled by the tyrannies of his king and employer, painted Saturn in the act of devouring one of his sons, an image described by Fred Licht as "essential to our understanding of the human condition in modern times".

Sarah Howe
from A Certain Chinese Encyclopedia

Belonging to the Emperor

Today my name is Sorrow.
So sang the emperor's first nightingale.

The emperor was a fickle god.
He preferred to be thrilled by an automatic bird

in filigreed gold. A musicbox, a leitmotif.
Love me, please. Orange blossom.

I see my father bathed in the blare of that same
aria, prodding the remote

to loop. *Chiamerà, chiamerà* –
His face is red. Beneath his glasses, it is wet.

Fabulous

> *GFP is a protein derived from the jellyfish* Aequorea victoria,
> *which emits green light upon illumination with blue light.*
> *– Hofker & van Deursen,* Transgenic Mouse: Methods and Protocols

Chimera, chimera –

     where does your garden grow?
A grafted Paradise. A mouthful of snow.

A Trojan conception – maculate cargo.
A spliced mouse – its unearthly day-glo.

James McGonigal
Towards Winter

for George Gordon in the Balkans

We were all forced to watch this, *reduced to silence*
as frost slowly wound its bandage round and round
the glen's face. Trees stood about the camp at dawn
like men not eager to try a back-breaking load. Still
wearing *remnants of their colours* for frost to stitch
or snow to bleach. We saw *village politics* in passing,
low sun hanging in its noose of cloud. Ten men died
just over there – sedition. Like a lochan where *swans*
swoop down to settle I became
a ghost of myself –

On that retreat we passed by twisted ranks of oak
with blood-stained dressings sticking to each limb.
Those were forced marches when our eyes *guarded*,
pricking like stars, flashed memories or figments –
till dawn leaked shadow on lintels, windows, cheek-
bones, brows. *Sharp mornings* when we looked for
the dying, lit breakfast fires and set smoke drifting
further than their cries. The drumskin of each page
on which stout pens beat white
black white black white –

Was it years? Fog spellbinds any road. By now
we had been sleepwalking for two hundred miles,
still far from sight of *the great indoors*: tableland,
hearth fires, a bed's undulating oceans or deserts.
What kept us apart was not distance, nor depth of
waves nor barren dust – destiny, that's all. And our
chief's blood, that was *meridian*, as if never cooled
by north-east winds. *Darkness had fallen* so fast
each tree in sheer fright dropped
handfuls of gold –

Underwater we rose through *one last dream* to grip
the sun's white arm. Lovers planted out. And *other
arrows* – saplings tall enough by now to launch their
flights of birds. Hedges caught in bryony, tight round
whatever's tall. There a boy and girl kissed. *Temperate*
between yew trees, led by berries and birdsong in shade
we followed one path. *Others go naked*. The old forest
was donning a brightly striped nightshirt. Trees waved
departing, their brown hands
thinner by the day.

Hilary Menos
Long Pig

We eat the flesh only in wartime, when enraged,
and in a few legal instances. Theft. Treason.

Adultery. When the elders deem fit, revenge.
When a captured prisoner cannot pay ransom

in coin or woman or pig. And we find nothing
animates missionaries like being eaten.

When we introduce you to the village elders,
you men, with your degrees from Oxford and Eton,

must squat at the far end of the hut from our king
due to your woeful lack of pigs. Still, be at ease.

But when our women gather salt, and limes, and rice,
hanging coconuts like sucked skulls from the palm trees,

it might be prudent to invoke the Lord's Prayer twice,
or whatever prayer, to whatever God you please.

David Wheatley
For Cosimo di Piero

Canvas is expensive and one who wastes
canvas on paintings not of the Bishop
of Bobo or the Countess of Caca
is an irresponsible person and you
are that person, abominating
the coughing of men and the chanting
of friars and making fifty boiled eggs
at a time. Vitruvius is telling you
how language was born: *when the trees*
caught fire, the men of old found
how pleasant the warmth was,
and trying to speak of this gave forth
sounds with differing intensity,
making customary by daily use
these random syllables. 'More beast
than man,' said Vasari: pyrophobe
who would set Eden ablaze and send
the beasts stampeding towards us,
lions, bears and aurochs punished
for not wanting rid, they too, of heaven
on earth. The forest is a furnace
but in the middle distance a goat
and deer with human faces pause
and ask themselves what to do: what
bodies, whose faces to wear,
they wonder, nature wonders,
flush with the wisdom of utter defeat
as a peasant of genius spells
'f – i – r – e, fire' for the first
time and the whole world burns down.

Sinéad Morrissey
Puzzle

for Sheila Llewellyn

Vitya pledges his brigade of Pioneers will plant
half as many fruit trees as the other Pioneers.
Kiryusha pledges *his* brigade, the best of the detachment,
will match the trees of all brigades together, including Vitya's.
Their brigades work the last shift simultaneously.
The preceding brigades of the detachment
plant forty trees. Both pledges are fulfilled exactly.
How many trees does the whole detachment plant?

Answer: a kind of Latin – finished and intricate,
or a box of plate-glass negatives from 1887
unearthed by accident of Newcastle cloth market.
The Oceanic Whitetip Shark. Ectoplasm.
Natasha Ivanova on her collective farm
working out the most efficient way to harvest cotton.

Tiffany Atkinson
Phallus Impudicus

That clarion stink. A death. Schlong-shroom! says Phil,
who spots it mooning through the tree-roots. The stink-
horn is hysterical with flies. Rebecca
    sickens with a sting

that overnight grows like a rose and all its
thorns across the right side of her face. Inside
the shady castle she turns softly on her
    histamines. Meanwhile

we itch for Coke and salty snacks and fall too
often into innuendo. One may talk
from seven p.m. Writing life is passive
    aggressive perhaps;

our loves and children have been disappointed
quietly in our quiet selfishness by
slow degrees, or not, and thrive on anyway
    despite, without us.

Given a month of outrageous privacy
what a mouthy collection of cells I am.
You wouldn't believe the stink of my exact
    indelible pains,

like the crab-juice that dripped through a paperback
during the long bus ride up. Murakami
I think. We have thrown him over the ramparts,
    unread; even so.

The stinkhorn has finished itself off and left
bare earth. It seems improbable like dream-sex,
though we heard its pale hoot travel the darkness –
    such a way to go.

(

what might have been said
in the night's eye's motorway caff
with one of those names
like Critchley Armageddon Services
where you propped your face
on coffee tight with sugar
and spoke of your marriage was

that sexuality is mostly a crystal
like the grit of sugar at the elbow
on a wipe-dry table or a minor abrasion
like Christmas and the coffee was good
which we stirred like people in grown-up
shoes so sweet our hands grew giddy
and the road home soft between the teeth

)

Chris McCabe
The Alchemist

Spoken by Lovewit who returns to the London he fled to escape the plague to find his home overrun with the ruses and deceptions of conmen Face, Subtle and Dol Common. Face wins a reprieve by stage-managing Lovewit's marriage with the woman he has fallen in love with, Dame Pliant. We are here, Blackfriars, 1610.

Will you be my speculatrix?   absence keeps us
guessing   this city can lick figs, I'll gum its silks
with cláy   *stuck full of black & melancholic worms*
    The old St Pauls was búrnt of trade & commerce
this hollow dóme's for confessions   blue was the life
motif for summer   & the youth you saw in my face
    London expells me twice weekly with plágue   the
provinces re-hearse my art   like a coal stuffed with
diamonds the wax splits at Eúston   the zòmbiés of
ambition   march policies of truth   but poets are
liars, the wind whórls their value phones   I'm on
loan with words of àccént rising   the terraces I've
come from   dictionary entries in duplicates
    definition FIRE licks my heels   Christ's blood in

carafes at business lunches   less toxic than sodium
glútamate   income enough to learn German   or go
back to therapy   Hoch Deutsch was not at Bábel   I
consort   with   the   small   poets   of   our   time
     the tooth fairy tweaks their nibs each night   and
milk leaks out each morning   When the bawd of
Lambeth meets the bard of Southwark   you get
another fuckin Revenger's play *This night, I'll change
all, that is metal, in thy house, to gold* even the
blàck fillings in this skull   that are rocks around the
skinned seal of the tongue.   if I show them when
I laugh   that's because to laugh is the anti-death
     even against the city's new plágue   named
COMMUTE   There is no travelcard to take us bàck

     I have a real toy sword but am in the wrong play
strung for a woman who circulates like oil   whórled
with rubber & roses   a *bonnibell*, the text said   a
soft & buxom widow   to this live skeleton
                    rattled with libido

Michael Hofmann
see something say something

every transparent man his own bar-
code his own passwords account
activity iris scan fingerprints
tribal / maiden name payment
history gold / silver / platinum /
lead cards ID (non-drivers incl.)
mobile number(s) email
addresses medical records
organ donor card insurance
allergies next of kin pets
police record age next birth-
day employer's letter tax
number implants joint re-
placements cranial plate
pacemaker social network
aliases chatrooms mother's
birthday and middle initial

welcome on board unusual
activity prior religious affili-
ation soul patch GSOH and smell

Alice Fulton
After the Angelectomy

And where my organ of veneration should be –
wormwood and gall. Grudge sliver.

Wailbone, iron, bitters. I mean to say the miniature
waterfalls have all dried up in this miniature

place where day is duty cubed, time is time on task
and every mind optimized for compliance.

Time to delint my black denim traveling stuff.
The florescent major highlighter has dimmed

to minor. I'm so dying I wrote
when I meant to write so tired.

And when I sleep I dream only that
I'm sleeping. Please see my black stuff's

dusted off. Night has no dilution anxieties,
but only the infinites are happy:

Math. Time. Everything happy goes
to many decimal places

while flesh passes through
gradations of glory. I visualized it,

the nurse said of the bedsore. Everything exists
at the courtesy of everything else.

Please see that my grave is kept clean.
Beloveds, finite things

in which the infinite endangered itself,
excarnate to memory and the divine substance

has limited liability. You're kind,
I tell the infinite. Too kind.

from Rondo for Singing Clock

Because We Never Practiced With The Escape Chamber

we had to read the instructions as we sank.
In a hand like carded lace. *Not nuclear warheads*
on the sea's floor nor the violet glow over the reactor
will outlive this sorrowful rhyme. Vain halo! My project
becalmed, I'll find I've built a monument
more passing than a breeze. It will cost us,
pobrecito. We can't buy a prayer. Did you call
my name or was that the floorboard
wheezing? These memories won't get any bigger,
will they? I think something is coming that will
vastly improve our quietude. I'm growing
snow crystals from vapor in anticipation and praying
for the velvet-cushioned kneeler that I need to pray.
I made this little sound for you to wait in.

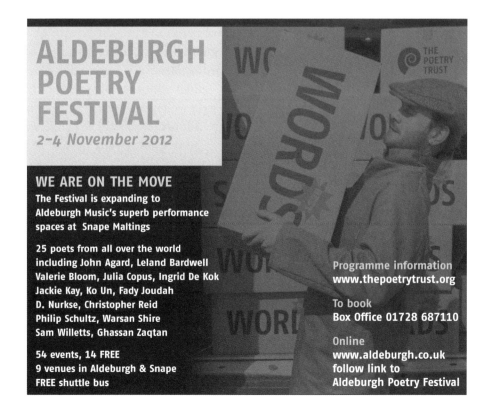

Dannie Abse
Talking to Myself

In the mildew of age
all pavements slope uphill

slow slow
towards an exit.

It's late and light allows
the darkest shadow to be born of it.

Courage, the ventriloquist bird cries
(a little god he is, censor of language)

remember plain Hardy and dandy Yeats
in their inspired wise pre-dotage.

I, old man, in my new timidity,
think how, profligate, I wasted time

    – those yawning postponements on rainy days,
    those paperhat hours of benign frivolity.

Now Time wastes me and there's hardly time
to fuss for more vascular speech.

The aspen tree trembles as I do
and there are feathers in the wind.

Quick quick
speak old parrot,
do I not feed you with my life?

Robin Fulton Macpherson
Hearing the Sea

Heard my blood say to my ear, "just me,"
and my tinnitus, "I never tire."

Dreamt that Acker Bilk played a tune called
"Leo Fibonacci on the shore".

There were many crushed whorls to tread on,
a few perfect to keep and measure.

Does hubris make whelks build such armour
their lives in slime can never outlive?

We give the whelks a pride they can't feel
and a cruelty that is all ours.

What if a godless dark once huddled
in, died from, the shell of York Minster?

There has been much interpretation
of the not-quite-silence that drowns out

footfalls and voices between such walls.
It's like the sea we don't hear in a conch.

C.J. Driver
An Interruption

i.m. Julia Swindells (1951–2011)

Depression did its worst. We might have guessed
That, when this world became a wood
Where tigers roam, retreating good
Would find itself entrapped by bad. The rest

We know too well. What else is there to say?
The printer's jammed, the ink run dry?
"Our kind" may mourn, but never cry?
In Yorkshire, understatement "rules the day"?

Her hands are poised above the piano keys;
It seems she can't decide which piece
To play. She turns to pull a face;
An eyebrow lifts as if she wants to quiz

An audience no longer there. We've gone
From her as she has gone from us;
And is this absence nothingness?

        What's done is done

And all the poems we'd hoped that we might hear
Are trapped between "delete" and "pause".
They circle in the air like crows
Disturbed by walkers on an upland moor.

Carrie Etter
My Mother's Ashes

I wanted to get naked, dip a finger
in water, dip a finger in you,
and paint my skin till
it was half me, half you in
a more accurate self-representation.
I wanted to upend the urn
like you said I toppled the sugar jar
at two: I reached up and its crystal grains
spilled over me, over the counter;
you walked in and I called, "Hi, Moddy,"
as though nothing were amiss.
(Nothing was.) In the night I wanted
to dig a hole in the back yard
and crawl in after you.
In the day I wanted to Victorianize,
have your ashes sealed in a clear
glass locket to rest an inch below
my larynx, a surrogate voice.
I wanted to sprinkle a little
into flour, egg and cocoa
and feed the cake of you to everyone.
I wanted to sit with my four sisters,
your twelve grandchildren, and say
"her own recipe" and "it's the best cake
I'll ever make."

John Hartley Williams
Still Grieving

On the flyblown mattress of the afternoon
everything's the same and nothing is.
January, I think, come down off your cross;
this clammy August is a fake.

The proper nouns, those dark propensities,
keep hooking gobbets of the real, and suddenly
I'm older by two minutes. Groucho Marx
has wandered in, like sunlight.

How did he get here? Time to probe
the stairwell's winding thesis and anti-
thesis. Time to stroll by the lake,
holding my pale girlfriend's hand.

It's been the wettest summer ever.
On the banks, the fishermen prop rods.
Do fish pay any mind to rain?
Something's tugging at my line.

Lights are going on in cafés.
Teeth clink on stealth-lifted teacups.
Sundays for sycophants! I want to shout.
See how the wreck goes down in flames!

Across the bay of teapots, the moon is rising.
Return from the dead, and I will too.
Let's discuss my girlfriend. The length of her skirt.
She doesn't speak much. You do.

A weak fog roIls off my chest.
I'm striding the lobby of the Hotel Neptune –
a fishmonger foist with a cry:
Spectral octopus! Get your spectral octopus here!

Tell me. The time before I was born.
What did you do without me? Who was that fellow on skis?
That smile in the photograph: for whom?
What were you trying to say, that last time?

Angelina Ayers
Days

It always comes down to this one early,
one patient and his Polish, his dementia,
the way his emaciating body founders
in the mattress pooling with faecal fluid

spilling from his stomach, the stoma bag
blown off, small intestine poking through,
a blooming crimson rose warm to the touch.

We look across the bed to one another
inadequate in aprons and gloves, soapy water
turning cold as we wonder where to begin,
then wade in, wrist deep and reassuring,

forgetting the intimacy, the oddness of it all,
our fingers reading ribs and ruckled scar,
a quiet language persisting between us.

Karen McCarthy Woolf
The Museum of Best-Laid Plans

(fragment)

Exhibit 17c (ii). Early 21st Century commonly adapted
bedside cabinet – Ikea, Billy shelving in beech veneer
containing a collection of miscellaneous domestic trinkets
and various homeopathic medicines (possibly placebo).
From bottom up: one transparent plastic watch (stopped);
Dr Bach Rescue Remedy (30ml dropper); calendula
thiossinaminum (6°), arnica, aconite; several paperback
books including a number of Pago-Christian materia medica
including *Sister Karol's Book of Spells and Blessings*;
Back to Eden; *African Holistic Health*, *The Fastest
Way to Get Pregnant Naturally*; and *Sonata Mulattica*
(poems). Shelves IV & V: containing 13 pairs of sunglasses
(designer and highstreet) ranging from imitation tortoiseshell
(origin Lagos, Nigeria: c.1974) to 1950s style bubblegum
pink rhinestone-studded (cf. early celebrity cultures partic.
An Audience with Dame Edna, 1986). Above: two boxes
ProJuven (1.5 & 3%) (empty) with folded instructions
*Applicare 1–2 misure di crema ogni giorno sulla zona
interna delta braccia...* Below: A4 stationery (Conqueror)
W Uden & Sons Ltd, Funeral Directors, labelled Infant:
Locks of Hair.

Edward Mackay
The Size of Wales

Half the Red
Sea / 381 Lochs
Ness / Mare Undarum
/ New York / New Jersey / Rhode Island /
291 million football pitches / 39 million fewer
rugby pitches / one hundred and thirty nine Halley's Comets / fifteen
days' circulation of *The Times of India* in a great paper mosaic /
The Falklands and Las Islas Malvinas / the Amazon
we lost this year / the Haitian quake's trembling
reach / 63 Argentinean lagoons / every inch of
Malawi with little to spare / enough solar panels
to light Western Europe / next year's expansion of
the Sahara Desert / a fifth of Canadian boreal forest
/ the asteroid that did in the dinosaurs / the teeming
Galapagos islands, twice / less than a sixth of England /
166 million Olympic swimming pools / enough coal for 300
years, and never the will to return to the mines / cloth to make the
proud red banners of twenty generations / a great lake of language,
each spoken word that's lost the ears that understand it / India's largest
mangrove swamp / the top half of Botswana/ Helmand Province / the lower
half of Botswana / every human ever born / fy mamwlad Cymru / two
thirds of Belgium / 20,779km² / the seepage from *Exxon Valdez* / 8,023 square
miles / every pot   hole in the western world / the unpublished
novels all needing a break / the things I used to
know / a fresh iceberg that will soon be the size of
the Isle of Man and none of it sandstone,
limestone, Cambrian gritstone or
deep black peat

Patrick Mackie
A Brief And Helpless Treatise
On The Subject Of The Heart

The tender evening light carried on shifting like a batch of hazy pigeons from
       rooftop
to rooftop before it finally settled. The charred shapes
of the colonnade, if that is the right word for it, breathed
calmly. I was waiting while a friend spoke
on the telephone to some colleagues and officials,
all of them trying to decide whether one of
her students should be committed or not to
a mental hospital. A few stars were nailing some thin clouds to the pale grey sky,
the weak teeth of the ivy whirred in the greyness,
and spoke. But they spoke in a foreign language. We are so
accustomed to so much failure when we attempt
to look into the minds of others that it is
all the more startling and frightening when we
abruptly succeed. Knowledge moved like a mist in the empty air,
so ashen and serene and comfortless,
a face on which the bright colours had burned themselves out. A library was
floating and whispering up above me, students were leaving
notes on coloured bits of paper in
their tiring copies of the same old tremendous classics,
beyond it roads stepped slowly away like yet more rough black thoughts trying
to inch away from themselves without anyone
noticing. The heart has no wings because it is a wing itself,
a single wing beating within the weakness of the flesh like a lake within its
       breaking
reflections, streaming as if it wanted to be able to
mount back up through the steep air like snow moving backwards
so as to throw its spreading shades back into their white beginnings. If
it should find another wing though,
it may be able to fly. Nearby,
a lake was rising out of itself like a tremulous grey eye.
I believe that this poem wants to be the reason why.

David Morley
World's Eye

far hid from the world's eye:
I fain would have some friend to wander nigh
                         — John Clare

My house hoves nowhere, hauled by invisible horses.
Shades shift around me, warming their hands at my hearth.
It has rained speech-marks down the windows' pages,
gathering a broken language in pools on their ledges
before letting it slither into the hollows of the earth.
My child stares out of windows on a pouring planet.
To him perhaps it is raining everywhere and forever.
I told myself this once. It is why I do not forget it;
although forty years have passed yet I am no older.
When Gypsy people speak aloud to one another
across greenway and hollow-way they say sister and brother.
When mother or father speak aloud to their children
they say our own daughter and they say our own son.
I call out to my child, and he is everywhere, and she is everyone.

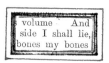

s volume   And
side I shall lie,
bones my bones

A HUMAN DOCUMENT.

A HUMAN DOCUMENT.

INTRODUCTION.

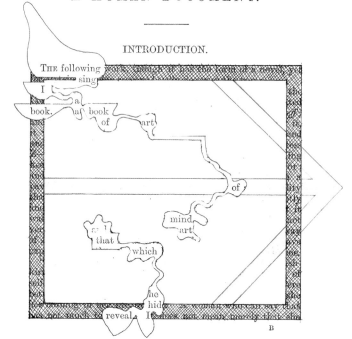

The following
sing
I
a
book,   a book   of   art

of

mind
art

that
which

he
hid
reveal. I

A Little White Opening Out of Thought

CHRIS MᶜCABE

Tom Phillips is a painter. He is also a printmaker, collagist and musician. In the 1980 edition of *A Humument: A Treated Victorian Novel* he stated in the introduction (which comes at the end of the book) that the process of using words found only in the text of an obscure Victorian novel to create his work provided "the solution for this artist of the problem of wishing to write poetry while not in the real sense of the word being a poet... he gets there by standing on someone else's shoulders."[1] Thirty-two years later, in the revised introduction to the fifth edition of the book, published this year, this reservation has been re-evaluated as Phillips talks of the "well over a thousand segments of poetry" he has created in the course of writing the five versions of the book. This maturing into himself as a poet chimes with developments within poetry over this same period of time to allow for a confident reassessment of Tom Phillips the Poet.

This is not to say *A Humument* is a straightforward book of poetry. Phillips cites Van Gogh and Blake as inspirations – both of whom walked the same streets of Peckham where Phillips first found the source book for his epic lifetime project in 1966. In a furniture repository facing Peckham Rye Phillips picked up *A Human Document* by W.H. Mallock after declaring to a friend that the first book he found for threepence would "serve a serious long-term project".[2] Where Blake was looking up into the trees for angels Phillips was among the deadwood of old furniture, trawling the books abandoned after house clearances. For an artist whose whole practice has thrived on chance and randomness this synchronicity with Blake is not lost. Blake's fusing of word and image (as well the decision to make artworks that would find their home in illustrated books) is as much a presence behind Phillips's work as the explosions of colour in the work of Van Gogh and Cezanne.

Of course the fusing of language with visual elements long precedes Blake, going back to the first formations of written languages in which script organically emerged as shapes that carried their meaning in the way they looked. Dick Higgins argues in *Pattern Poetry: Guide to an Unknown*

---

1. Tom Phillips, *A Humument*, Thames and Hudson, 1980.
2. Tom Phillips, *A Humument*, Thames and Hudson, 2012.

Literature that the instinct to take pleasure from works that contain both word and image is a human instinct that goes back to roots of both Western and Eastern cultures: "an ongoing human wish to combine the visual and literary impulses".[3] *A Humument* works in this tradition, satisfying the subterranean stirrings within us to have our visual and literary senses satisfied in one almighty fix. A few years back at an exhibition at the Saison Poetry Library by Sam Winston, a text-based artist who works with intricate deconstructions of canonical works – fairy tales, Shakespeare, the dictionary – it was noticeable how those with visual art backgrounds began their viewing by standing well back to assimilate the overall form, whilst those comfortable with poetry walked straight up to the pieces to read the words. As most of us are let down by the narrowness of our training in our specialist areas we should be grateful to artists like Tom Phillips and Sam Winston who play around with the spaces between our senses, the habits we form when looking at art and the world around us.[4]

What is *A Humument*, this constantly revised book that Phillips has been working on since 1966? His creative process involves painting, drawing or collaging over the original pages of text in the novel until just a little of the text is visible through the new images on the page. Words determine the visual direction. In one sense this parallels what a poet does through choosing words available in the language – or the book of the language, the dictionary – and creating the best order for those words (poets also make new words, as does Phillips, though his available source book, a single novel, is infinitely smaller than the English dictionary). In a poem all the unused words are invisible, their invisibleness determining the impact of the words chosen on the page. In *A Humument*, where the words are selected from those present on the page of the novel, sometimes the unselected words are still semi-visible beneath paint.

Phillips the painter never begins with a clean canvas; Phillips the poet never begins with a clean page. The Oulipo approach to making literature from restrictions provides another line in the tradition of experimentation through which to consider Phillips's place in poetry. A work such as Raymond Queneau's *One Hundred Million Million Poems*, in which each line appears on a strip of paper, works similarly to *A Humument* in the way the constriction determines the possibility for an almost endless sequence of new poems to be created. On three pages in the new edition Phillips manages to make, across the space of a few lines, the exclamation: "O | C | e | z | an | n | e".

3. Dick Higgins, *Pattern Poetry: Guide to an Unknown Literature*, State University of New York Press, 1987, p.3
4. To view Sam Winston's work go to samwinston.com; artists within the same collective – Victoria Bean and Karen Bleitz – are at arceditions.com.

Phillips has talked of how for years he has hoped that the book could be used as a kind of oracle, accessed at random to offer cryptic snippets of life-advice and portent.[5] The App version for the iPhone and iPad particularly delighted him because as well as a random access feature it also has a facility to draw together two pages side-by-side and to light them through the screen like "church windows".[6]

The argument that Phillips is a poet will receive little resistance from those associated with the second wave of concrete poetry and the US-influenced experimental group often referred to as the British Poetry Revival of the 1960s. While the first wave of concrete poets in the 1950s aspired to a minimal purity, the second wave were more heterogeneous and sprawling in their experiments, and Phillips's early work on *A Humument* was embraced by the editors of the magazines arising from this movement. Pages from *A Humument* appeared in magazines such as *Arlington*, *Exit* and *Stereo Headphones*, and alongside concrete poets such as John Furnival, Dom Sylvester Houédard and Eugen Gomringer. One page – representing one of several aesthetic strands that recur throughout the book – has been created by simply typing red and black Xs, Zs and Cs over the original page of the novel and is redolent of a Dom Sylvester Houédard typestract. An initial short version of *A Humument* called *trailer* was published in 1971 by Hansjörg Mayer, whose *futura* series of broadsides included Edwin Morgan, Bob Cobbing and Ian Hamilton Finlay. In an issue of the magazine *Ginger Snaps* ("a collection of cut-ups / machine prose / word & image") from 1972 an early Xeroxed black-and-white page from *A Humument* was published with explanatory text from Phillips citing William Burroughs as an influence. In *British Poetry Magazines 1914–2000* Geoffrey Hill – a near exact contemporary of Phillips – is cited for publication in eleven magazines, while Phillips follows closely behind with eight.[7] The present edition of *A Humument* is dedicated to Ruth and Marvin Sackner, concrete poetry collectors who in 1975 founded the Sackner Archive, a home for Phillips's work.

By the time Phillips had begun *A Humument* in 1966 there was a significant crossover between the international movement of concrete poetry and the US-led Fluxus (which, like most of the significant movements of the time, had poets at its core). The experiments of John Cage (whom Phillips

5. I was reading the new edition on a train from Liverpool to London on the first day of the *Poetry Parnassus* festival on the Southbank and came across this page: "days | of | poetry |...Tickets ready – for | Liverpool | and | expectancy".
6. Tom Phillips quoted in the *Observer*, 20 May 2012.
7. David Miller and Richard Price, *British Poetry Magazines 1914–2000: A history and bibliography of 'little' magazines*, The British Library, 2006. This is not a complete number of how many magazines both poets appeared in during this period.

cites as an inspiration) in using random operators such as the *I Ching* were also providing process-led inspiration for poets such as Jackson Mac Low. When Dick Higgins invented the phrase 'intermedia' in 1965 it was almost a label-fit for what Phillips was about to embark upon. Phillips has gone on to use the same source text to create an opera, *Irma*, and to append his own artworks. He has also translated Dante with a commentary using words from the same source text.

By 2012 we should be untroubled by the idea of accepting a poet who works with found materials as a genuine poet. It was over a century ago when Duchamp entered a urinal into an art competition. Yet the stakes are higher with language, particularly within English Literature – despite decades of experimentation and questioning of what poetic integrity and 'inspiration' might mean, many readers remain unconvinced that poems made from words that already exist in another, often more mundane form can be real poems. The American poet and founder of UbuWeb Kenneth Goldsmith has been influential in steering forward this alternative approach through his own conceptual poetry – and the championing of others – in the US. The Flarf movement's trawling of the internet's digital bladderwrack for found poetry is done in the same spirit as Phillips began his epic forty years before. The controversy caused by Goldsmith's approach in books like *Fidget* – in which every movement of his body is recorded over a three-day period – lies not just in the conceptual idea but in Goldsmith's assertion that his books don't actually need to be read.[8] Many of Goldsmith's influences are the same as Phillips's – in *Against Expression*, co-edited by Goldsmith, he also includes writings by William Burroughs and John Cage.[9]

Phillips too delights in the found. Aside from *A Humument* being entirely based within the words of a randomly-found book, Phillips often chooses the text he will work with by tossing a coin over the page of the novel; the project's very title came from folding over two pages of the novel until the original title, *A Human Document*, became *A Humument*. But the idea of *A Humument* is only the prefix to what happens on its pages. You couldn't tell someone about *A Humument* – as strong as the idea is – and not want to show them the work. *A Humument* is not a book to know about, it is a book to delight in – for its colour, for the constant surprise, for the open-ended play of language. There is a massive investment of authorial

---

8. Kenneth Goldsmith defines the new conceptual poetry as "fusing the avant-garde impulses of the last century with the technologies of the present, one that proposes an expanded field for 21st century poetry" (poetryfoundation.org/harriet/2008/06/conceptual-poetics-kenneth-goldsmith).
9. *Against Expression: an anthology of conceptual writing*, ed. Craig Dworkin and Kenneth Goldsmith, Northwestern University Press, 2011.

intervention: a page may be worked on over years, only to be amended or rewritten for a new edition. Phillips is both a conceptual, or process, poet – whose whole project (lasting most of his life) has been based around a book found by chance (what if he had found a different novel that day?) – and also the craftsman of finished masterpieces. His process of amendment and revision has a compelling tension between Audenesque revision and auto-destruction. There is no such thing, and never will be, as a final, completed version of *A Humument*. It is a monster that devours his creativity (he claims that he's worked through eight copies of *A Human Document* but has never read the book in a linear way from start to finish) but never gets significantly bigger.

The artworld is comfortable with embracing the entirety of Phillips's work as art, so why should the poetry world (and this is his second appearance in *Poetry Review*) not embrace him as a poet? He has both exhibited and curated at the Royal Academy, yet very little has been said about his gift as a poet. If Goldsmith is right, it is time to accept that we have had our Duchamps in poetry and that poets working in this tradition are genuine poets. Phillips abounds with the skills of selecting, cutting, and positioning words with a flair for rich connections and memorable synchronicities. Reading his words is to be compelled by his tuning of every metrical stress in the words selected for use on his pages:

> wanted. a little white opening out of thought

This is a line that Phillips plucked randomly from *A Human Document* in 1974 when he was looking for texts to append to paintings. It shows his focus on the minimal, gathering clusters of words that work with a lower-case allusive charge (the "wanted" left hanging from the sentence gives the line instant impact), with a condensed Imagist clarity.[10] *A Humument* is an epic of minimal poems. There are similarities with Charles Olson's *Maximus Poems*: Phillips walked the streets of Peckham as Olson did in Gloucester, Massachusetts, to find the source for his epic. A page in the new edition shows a map of Peckham Rye with the lines "the gallery of a | hundred years | of | a thousand | is in | every street". There is also a parallel between Olson's focus on the Projective use of space (or Open Field) and Phillips's use of what he calls "rivers" – the white bubble-clouds drawn around each section

---

10. Pound's three *Prefaces to the Imagists* written between 1913 and 1916 prove a useful way of measuring Phillips's success as a poet: point after point seems to be carried out by Phillips, particularly "To use absolutely no word that did not contribute to the presentation". *Imagist Poetry*, introduced and edited by Peter Jones, Penguin, 1972.

of words to show the order in which they should be read. Perhaps a closer comparison would be with Olson's friend and contemporary at Black Mountain College, Robert Creeley – a collection like *Pieces* draws on the particles of words and the resulting emphasis on breath that we also find in Phillips. In fact reading aloud some of Phillip's words is the best measure of its flow and impact as poetry – it is often beautiful in both music and image: "At last felt her | forest. | dearer to him now than | broken syllables which | are for lovers signs". The alert attunement to the syllable puts Phillips firmly in the American Poundian tradition (with echoes too of William Carlos Williams) through Olson to contemporaries such as Rachel duPlessis (poets all tuned in to the metrics of poetic language as well as working in epics). The closest poet to Phillips in England is Tom Raworth: parallels can be drawn not only between the focus on language particles but also in the humour and pastiching of the English middle class and academia (literary in Raworth's case, in Phillips the artworld – which gets a hammering in this edition). These lines from the new edition, detailing what happened to the character Toge on Hampstead Heath, could be a short Raworth poem: "the | Bible | a | newspaper | and | some | opaque | British idea | saved him".

Some of the most memorable pages in the book come about when Phillips is almost commenting on his own work: "listen | to the | sound of | the colour of a flower | It is enough | listen". Many of these pages even have a title, almost as if they are consciously being presented as poems – one is entitled COME AUTUMN HAND (an anagram of *A Human Document*), with lines worthy of *The Waste Land*: "as | gene-making | men | doctor | the land | composed of anxiety and | financial earth" (this is set against the stunning backdrop of auburn leaves over an azure blue). Writing of London, Phillips assembles word clusters that condense the grime and energy of the metropolis into very few words: "Compared with | London, all | shadowland; and the numb | who shuffled round | work | ville | helpless". His ear is attuned to the turn of each syllable, each phoneme – "Turn to | serious, | syllables" – being comfortable both in breaking words into particles and creating sounds and sense that keep each page alert to dreamlike unfolding narrative. It is this shifting of gears within language which makes *A Humument* such a lively reading experience – Phillips uses rhyme in one place, cryptic parataxis in another; a proverbial generalisation can easily shift to fragmentation and distortion. As readers we are constantly having our expectations played with.

Working with a language condensed with Pound's metrical emphasis on the syllable, Phillips is comfortable with particles, stranded letters. His concentrated allusiveness is easily read within the tradition of developments in Modernism to J.H. Prynne and beyond: "numb | winter | lust | unable to |

come to | candles. | drew aside from | white | age,". He has an assured command over the elasticity of language, even delving into sound poetry – as in this page exploring Toge's subconscious: "actica | plete", "gement | ong", "houl | atter", "ometh | ribble". He is capable of the pitch-perfect lyric poem – like this, which echoes the style of Celan: "chance memories. | a | violet | shadow | -lily I have walked by in | the dark". He often hacks and compounds words in a way that recalls Hopkins: "from the numb | avenue of | utter | love... she | ill-mended, and | he | just | by rust | down-drawn". And we can trust that Phillips knows what he is up to as the whole book is littered with references to – and echoes of – the work of other poets. The very first words of the new edition have a Whitmanesque reverb: "I | sing | a | book". A direct quote from Mallarmé is arranged inside a porthole: "a throw of dice will never do away with chance". Eliot's Prufrock is pastiched towards the end of the book ("-let us | go | now"), as well as *The Waste Land*: "in London | thronging | faces had no | friends | I | had | not | known | so | many".

In this revised fifth edition there are significant additions and reopenings. Phillips has employed photomontage to powerful effect, especially in relation to text about London crowds. Developments since 1980 have allowed for meanings to be gleaned that wouldn't have been possible before: through technology ("her face | book"; "The | app | of this volume"; "text | him | now"); through politics ("remember | bush |... that | bitter | name"): through colour – many pages are lit in red, pink, purple, bermuda green that are far brighter than previous editions. There is more self-referentiality in this edition, a looking-back on past experiences of women and having children. As the 1892 of W.H. Mallock continuously recedes, *A Humument* asks to be reworked in ways that would not have been possible before; and as the language base Phillips has to draw upon from the outside world has deepened in the years of the project, so too have the poet's gifts. In this new edition the "wanted" from the 1974 line quoted above has been replaced with the more assertive: "Here is art | coming to | claim" – a suitable shift for a poet declaring his own self-fulfilment in the arrival of the work which was promised forty-five years before: "Here is art | coming to | claim | a little white | opening out of | thought".

Chris McCabe's THE RESTRUCTURE was published by Salt this year. A sequence of Jacobean poems (see page 17) will be published in the anthology *Dear World & Everyone In It: New Poetry in the UK* (Bloodaxe, 2012) and later as a pamphlet with Egg Box / F.U.N.E.X.

From Page to Stage

CHRISSY WILLIAMS

"Risk. Audiences love it. Audiences don't know the rules. Because there aren't any." – Poet Hannah Silva on writing for theatre

Poetry is migrating into performative territory – the theatre. This may seem like a natural progression, or regression, considering poetry's roots in an oral tradition stretching back millennia. And yet poetry in the theatre is often still perceived as novelty, as a watering down of text, as adding a layer of artifice to something which should be connected with the eye, in silence, in privacy. These assumptions lack insight into the innovative ways in which poets are taking their words to the stage, and the intensity with which poetries may be experienced in a totally different form.

Martin Figura's *Whistle*, which has been touring theatres up and down the country since 2010, is a sequence of poems which was originally published in book form by Arrowhead Press, but which has also been developed and enhanced, in the hands of Apples and Snakes producer Sarah Ellis, with audiovisual elements (actors' voice recordings, music, images projected onto a screen), to create a poetry "experience" on a theatre stage. Central to *Whistle* is the story of Figura's parents, his mother's death at the hands of his father, but the piece dwells less on the act itself than on the negative space around it, the absence and loss of his mother, the loss of childhood innocence. On this point it speaks of a more general experience with which many different audiences can connect. On stage, Figura moves between two microphones, while a projector behind shows a range of small animations, real family photographs and images recalled from Figura's childhood, keepsakes and artefacts from his youth. Figura's reading is interspersed with lines from other voices, the actors or recordings unseen. The emphasis is on Figura, his words, his story.

This experience revolves firmly around the text. The projections neither question nor need interpreting; they complement and embellish, opening the door into Figura's childhood a little wider, rooting the work in reality to make it more intense. Childhood comics are laid over a photo of terraced houses on Figura's street. The effect created is one of visual scrapbook, animated enough to be more than images on a page, a companion to the show rather than a film in its own right.

A more performative example of this sort of approach is the recent *Kalagora* show, written and performed by Siddhartha Bose and produced by Penned in the Margins. The professional sound and lighting design set the stage, with a score written by Bollywood composer Pankaj Awasthi accompanying a film projected onto the back wall in snippets. This punctuates the performance, its own internal narrative complementing the text but also enjoyable without it, a development of the role multimedia plays in the performance. While *Whistle* revolves closely around the poet's story, *Kalagora* develops further an understanding of the poet as performer. In a previous generation, Larkin famously disliked poetry readings because he felt he was "impersonating himself". Here, that putdown is turned on its head to enhance, not diminish, the work.

Using multimedia elements which take on a life of their own creates quite different effects. *The Debris Field*, created by Simon Barraclough, Isobel Dixon and Chris McCabe to mark the centenary of the sinking of the Titanic, involves a live reading by the three poets while a specially commissioned film plays continuously before the audience, an element (albeit a more abstract one) in its own right. There is also a soundtrack created and performed for the project by Bleeding Heart Narrative's Oli Barrett. From an audience's perspective, the most immediate difference between *The Debris Field* and *Whistle* is the positioning of the poets themselves. While Martin Figura took centre stage for *Whistle*, in the two *Debris Field* performances given so far the poets were out of sight, so that the visual focus was the film itself. This results in a strangely hypnotic and immersive experience. With the poets absent, with no eye contact or visual connection between them and the audience, each word speaks to us more directly, whispered into our ears by ghosts. The text itself is dense and demanding. We become less interested in the person or persona of the poet and more focused on the work itself.

A simpler use of the stage, without multimedia, is exemplified by Julia Bird's touring poetry performances with her live literature company Jaybird, which uses directed readings and atmospheric lighting designs to bring poets to new theatre audiences that the printed page by itself may not have reached. The work of Live Canon, an ensemble of professional actors and theatre-makers who perform poetry's back catalogue, touring classic poetry from previous centuries, raises interesting questions about whether the integrity of the work is compromised by its being voiced in public not by the author but by actors. In what way is an actor's reading of a poem less "authentic" than the poet's? Glyn Maxwell, both poet and playwright, talks about making what he calls "poets' theatre" in *Magma*'s "Putting on the Mask" issue, advising poets to "go and find a space and some actors. Test your verse on the lungs and throats and tongues and lips of creatures trained to know utterance from nonsense."

The *Golden Fables* project, part of this year's Cultural Olympiad, is a poetic drama on stage and film, fused with music, with specially written words from Archbishop Desmond Tutu, Ian McMillan, Gillian Clarke, Liz Lochhead and Joel Stickley. This format, this medium, this combination of words, performance and staging (often with multimedia elements) is being increasingly recognised and encouraged as a method to engage new audiences. The delineation between page and stage no longer exists in the same way that it once did. Even the term "performance poet", as a way of distinguishing those poets whose poems simply work better when recited or performed from those whose work is intended to be read exclusively on the page, is collapsing – if it means simply a poet who is an excellent public reader of his or her work, then Geoffrey Hill is one such: his banter between poems would do Tommy Cooper proud.

One recent performance which incorporated all the elements mentioned above was *Shad Thames, Broken Wharf*, a play for voices written by poet Chris McCabe and produced for the London Word Festival by Tom Chivers. This incorporated a live orchestra and film projection, as well as a live performance from the poet at the start, with the bulk of the work then read by two actors. The poet was both present and absent, the work was both poem and performance, revolving around words, interacting with multimedia, all of which took on lives of their own while combining to create a springboard of connections for the audience to interpret and explore.

This isn't about replacing books with curtain calls. I'm not arguing that a poetry audiovisual "experience" is somehow *better* than the experience of reading poetry on the page. This essay is simply a flag, saying "look over here, look at all these interesting projects which are springing off the page and into our faces. These are performances, experiences, a new medium for communication." Because text in performance stops being pure page text and becomes something else, which is experienced in a different way, poets more familiar with poetry on the page may be more aware of the risks than the possibilities offered by the stage. But as the poet, performer and theatre-maker Hannah Silva noted in the quote that opens this essay, audiences don't see it that way. Talking about her own writing in the same blogpost from which that quote is taken, she continues: "The page is only the first breath."

Chrissy Williams's pamphlet *The Jam Trap* was published earlier this year. A Happen*Stance* pamphlet is due in 2013. She works at the Poetry Library and teaches at the Poetry School.

ℬ

Compendium in Time

KATY EVANS-BUSH

Adventures in Form, ed. Tom Chivers, Penned in the Margins,
£9.99, ISBN 9781908058010
Glyn Maxwell, *On Poetry*, Oberon Books, £12.99, ISBN 978184943

The Shakers, that American sect famous for their simple, beautiful furniture and textiles, had a saying: "Every force evolves a form." This speaks of two things: one, a fundamental respect for the integrity of the made object. And two, an understanding of the kinetic, the physical, origins of its making; in fact, of its transition from idea to object.

In the beginning the force was exerted. Dai Vaughan, the distinguished film editor and writer who died earlier this year, prefaced one of his books with words from Ernst Toller: "What we call form is love."

With the books under review here, two powerful kinetic forces in British poetry have exerted their force on the notion of "form". We're long overdue a serious consideration of form (which is, after all, only the opposite of chaos) that looks beyond the tired saw of rhyming/metrical vs not-rhyming/metrical. "Form" has for ages somehow been seen as a sort of veneer, something that's tacked on to make some kind of point, as if there were nothing left under the surface of postmodernism. An interest in structure has been enough to label someone "conservative", as if it were a political matter.

Tom Chivers, publisher of Penned in the Margins books, has edited a radical anthology of poems showing "how form can be employed as a framework for innovation", intending it to act as "a bestiary of exotic textual creatures". In it, poems by 46 poets – from arch-experimentalists like Christian Bök and Theodore Chiotis to polymaths Ruth Padel and George Szirtes, via Oulipians, epistolarians, and various kinds of code – provide a glimpse into a world of poetry teeming with life of all kinds, with a dazzling array of plumage and toothery and mating cries. Here's another quote, from Paul Muldoon: "Form is a straitjacket the way a straitjacket was a straitjacket for Houdini." So *Adventures in Form* is, among other things, a compendium of daring escapes.

Glyn Maxwell's book *On Poetry* seems, in contrast, a quiet enough thing. It's intensely personal – a sort of combination teaching guide, polemic and discursive philosophy of what poetry is, in particular what form is – and what it's for. But don't be fooled: it's as highly charged as a stick of poetry dynamite, blowing everything out and starting again from first principles. The first two chapters are called "White" and "Black". "Let's start with poetry's inventions that are absolutely required", Maxwell writes, taking a point from Aristotle: "their names are something and nothing..."

> Poets work with two materials, one's black and one's white. Call them sound and silence, life and death, hot and cold, love and loss; any can be the case but none of these yins and yangs tell the whole story. What you feel the whiteness is right now – consciously or more likely some way beneath that plane – will determine what you do next. Call it this and that, whatever it is this time, just don't make the mistake of thinking the white sheet is nothing... For a poet it's everything.

For Maxwell, the white is time. In the next chapter, "Black", he writes:

> In my work the white is everything but me, and the black is me... All I believe, and therefore all I teach... is that the form and tone and pitch of any poem should coherently express the presence of a human creature. Content, matter, subject, these all play little part. Form plays almost every part, which is why I continue to say that who masters form masters time.

This notion of time is integral to the book. The poems, the forms, that last are the ones that move within its elements in what Maxwell calls a "creaturely" way. The living presence is there on the page, in black and white. Time, he says, is our enemy. Who masters form masters time. And he re-envisages poetry as a synaesthesiac struggle between the black and the white, where the white presses in on the black, shaping it, and the black exerts its force on the white...

Which brings us back to *Adventures in Form*, with its creatures crouching in black and white on the field of our own particular time. Both these books are beautifully stripped-back, black-and-white productions, with absolutely says-it-on-the-tin chapter headings: in Maxwell, "Black", "White", "Form", "Pulse", "Space", and so on. In *Adventures in Form*, "Found Materials"; "Txts, Tweets and Status Updates"; "N+7"; "Emergent"; "Code is Poetry". In "Traditional Revised", sonnets and sestinas get the spam and breakbeat treatment. Maxwell says, "Certain forms abide, and it ought to fall to each new generation to master them, rework them for the times. Otherwise they enervate and wither, and you see poets turning back to a kind of defensive formalism born of nostalgia." (This happened with the Georgians, too; not just the New Formalists.) And so, this book contains at least one cento, a "found" form that originated in Ancient Rome and was popular during the Renaissance. It has a sestina, several sonnets, a poem in two columns based on Anglo-Saxon alliterative form (though without alliteration), investigations of translation, and an ancient Celtic form updated.

It also contains many poems written in forms that seem to speak more about the poet's process than about the shape of the object – the *force* at work. Randomisers range from classic Oulipo N+7 (now 50 years old) to predictive text messaging, to lines painted on the backs of sheep and rearranged according to where the sheep went. Several poets-worth of "invented" forms, where a poet imposes more and more arcane limitations on himself, demonstrate varying degrees of success. Some of them don't really appear to be forms at all – just poets with some sort of structural rationale. Poems shaped as correspondence don't strike me as a very revolutionary concept (*Pamela*, Samuel Richardson's benchmark epistolary novel, was published about a mile from Penned in the Margins, in 1740) and some of these seemed a bit thin – not very *compressed*, as the mainstream crowd might say. The danger, in several sections of the book, is of foregrounding what looks like (but may not really be) novelty. The poem has to outlast the trick of it.

But this book is full of delights and challenges. It watches poets – established, young, "mainstream", "experimental" – as they seek to hew something new and meaningful out of the old rock. Out of, as Glyn Maxwell calls the iambic pentameter (which several of these poets write in), "this magnificent engine of English poetry". It shows that the choice absolutely isn't about being *either* New Formalist *or* "without form, and void". That being experimental, on some terms or other, is common to every poet, to every poem ever written. Even the poems written in – or partly in – computer code are creaturely and poetic – in particular Chris McCabe's 'Recession'. (Many of these poems seem to operate via accumulation and transformation; they're very hard to quote the odd line from.)

Highlights include: Chrissy Williams's 'The Lost', made out of various translations of the opening of *The Divine Comedy*. George Ttoouli's haunting 'May Day', from 'Three Warnings'. Paul Muldoon's 'Eating Chinese Food in a Straw Bale House, Snowmass, Colorado, January 2011'. Ross Sutherland's Oulipo Red Riding Hood, 'The Liverish Red-Blooded Riffraff Hooha' (which reminds me of Howard Chace's homophonic *jeu d'esprit*, 'Ladle Rat Rotten Hut', written in 1940). Paul Stephenson's 'Family Values', a reworking of a potted bio of Carol Vorderman. Simon Barraclough's 'Manifest'. Christian Bök's masterly sequential translation of Rimbaud's 'Voyelles':

O , the supreme Trumpeter of our strange sonnet –
quietudes crossed by another [World and Spirit],
O, the Omega! – the violet raygun of [Her] Eyes...

'Voyelles', by the way, gets a name-check in *On Poetry*, too, in a statement that takes on layers of meaning (like synaesthesiac impressions?) as one continues to think about it: "I'd certainly have failed Arthur Rimbaud for writing that poem called 'Voyelles' in which he calls 'A noir, E blanc, I rouge, U vert, O bleu'. Amateur. Anyone knows it's A yellow, E blue, I white, O black, U purple. What do you think it is? Please don't say. Maybe synaesthesia is something one does alone."

Like the bestiary Tom Chivers calls it, *Adventures in Form* teems with life. It is the start of a new, healthier and more joyous way of looking at the poetic endeavour we live among. It's essential reading right now, and I hope there will be sequels.

As for Glyn Maxwell's book, there are a handful of books about writing that I count among my indispensible texts: by Guy Davenport, Randall Jarrell, Durs Grünbein, Keats, Pound, Brodsky, Virginia Woolf, Fanny Burney, Eliot. I knew on about page two that this book was one of them.

In the full spirit of Glyn Maxwell's black-on-white creature, here is Hannah Silva conquering time, in her text-speak 'Grecian Urn' poem, 'a mo ina _/ jar':

... Go get her m8. &he did.
Didn't you? As if dat wz it,
dat simpl. u thort, 1day n d
fucha der wl B a _/ jar on a
countA in a rm dat l%ks lk
u n l%ks lk M2n dat jar wl
contain ll deez moments,
n d mist swirls arnd em,
n we'll smhw B preserved.

Katy Evans-Bush is the author of *Me and the Dead* and *Egg Printing Explained* (Salt) and *Oscar & Henry* (Rack Press). She writes the blog Baroque in Hackney, and teaches poetic form at the Poetry School in London.

℘

Technical Virtuosi

HELENA NELSON

Clive James, *Nefertiti in the Flak Tower: Collected Verse 2008–2011*,
Picador, £14.99, ISBN 9781447207009;
James Fenton, *Yellow Tulips: Poems 1968–2011*, Faber, £14.99,
ISBN 9780571273829

These two books are members of the same club. Both are hard-backed; both demy 8vo in size; both have smart blue jackets. Author names loom top left and they're the same size (huge). CLIVE JAMES flashes in gold; JAMES FENTON glitters in yellow (to match his tulips). Inside, the paper is good: off-white, nice texture. The typeface is, if not identical, remarkably similar, though Fenton commands a bigger point size. Each poet – a bizarre replication – is praised in the blurb for "technical virtuosity". (Remember *Some Like it Hot*? – "every girl in my band is a virtuoso and I intend to keep it that way".)

But they *are* virtuous, both of them. It's easy to find poems to like in either volume, though Fenton's book is twice as thick, so theoretically the choice is greater (James packs 46 poems into 86 pages; Fenton has only 57 in 164). If you want to read Clive James, you can find most of the poems on his website. If you want Fenton, buy the book.

One crucial and obvious difference between the two poets (apart from age) is the business of television. With a major TV personality, the voice and face are unforgettable. I can't read Clive James in prose without experiencing his speaking voice: I *relish* the way he writes and speaks. In his verse, the poetic "voice" often falls short of expectation. To some extent, it seems to me, he uses form to create "poetic" diction, to define how Clive James sounds in verse, as opposed to the Other Clive James. His prose cadences are over-written by metre, usually iambic. This feels either comforting (depending where you stand on matters of metre) or relentless. I'd say a bit of both. Here are the opening lines of 'Language Lessons':

> She knew the last words of Eurydice
> In every syllable, both short and long.
> Correcting his misuse of quantity,
> She proved the plangent lilt of Virgil's song
> Depended on precision...

Nothing much to complain about there. The lines are fine, if slightly mind-numbing. But where's the Clive James voice that never ever bores? I don't mean he has "mastered his technique... but... not to the extent of being able to take liberties with it", as Eliot said of Swinburne. Sometimes he *does* achieve the magic formula – that special blend of form and feeling – and then the poem takes off (for my money, 'Vision of Jean Arthur and the Distant Mountains' is a winner). But often he doesn't.

A warning sign is profusion of the relative pronoun "that", popular in iambic pentameter, cordially loathed in radio scripting. In 'Pennies for the Shark', for example, there's "Suspecting *that* she might be sick of things, / *That* shark, in slow pursuit..." (italics mine). In a script, you'd cut the first "*that*" and increase the drive. Another sign of "poetic" diction is the way speech contractions dwindle. In 'A Perfect Market', for example:

> But on the whole it's useless to point out
> That making the thing musical is part
> Of pinning down what you are on about.

"It's useless" is good. It's brisk; it's Clive James. But – "what you are on about"? *Nobody* says that. The correctness of the metrical pattern dulls the poet's ear to lines that – while they may be said to work formally – do not function effectively in any other sense.

I would like more of the Other Clive James in the poetry. It can be done formally: I'm not pleading for *vers libre*. And he can do it. I found 'Vertical Envelopment', about the poet's recent illness, moving, convincing and effective. Here's the opening (the rest is on his website). It sounds just like Clive James:

> Taking the piss out of my catheter,
> The near-full plastic bag bulks on my calf
> As I drag my I.V. tower through Addenbrooke's
> Like an Airborne soldier heading for D-Day
> Down the longest corridor in England.

Those who think we have lost touch with metre and form (I am not one of them), will be comforted by this collection. It is not, however, "technical virtuosity" that singles out the best pieces. It's something rarer.

James Fenton is also a virtuoso of prosody. He's a far more varied writer, though, and as he switches from one mode to another, there's a feeling of relaxed largesse. I was reminded, severally, of Bob Dylan, Stevie Smith, Louis

MacNeice, W.H. Auden, Wendy Cope, Adrian Mitchell and Charles Causley. But of course he's nothing like any of them.

Perhaps his self-evident strength – the consummate ease with which he works form, tone and line – can also have drawbacks. In the early poem, 'Children in Exile', which extends over nine pages, I'd lost attention by page three. Fenton could probably go on with balladic quatrains forever, but he might not always take his reader with him. He does brief poems too, needless to say, and long poems with some brief sections, like 'Manila Manifesto'. But I don't find the lines "We call on America to stop killing, torturing and / imprisoning its poets" funny enough for a whole costly Faber & Faber page. That's the trouble with witty writing: it's a matter of taste. I like James Fenton best when he summons aching simplicity, as in his final poem, 'Rain':

> They stretch a torn sail taut between torn hands
> To fill the pail.
> They turn their channelled faces to the sky
> And the sweet rain runs in their eyes
> And on the channelled sea.

Yellow Tulips is an excellent volume for readers encountering this poet for the first time. From the wonderful early poem 'Wind' (you can hear him read it on the Poetry Archive) to the recent 'Yellow Tulips', the verse is charged with energy. No question about that: the book crackles. Fenton doesn't try to please. He does what pleases *him*, and he does it inimitably.

Helena Nelson is the founder editor of Happen*Stance* Press. Her latest collection, *Plot and Counter-Plot*, was published by Shoestring Press in 2010.

Slightly Bad Boys

JAMES SUTHERLAND-SMITH

Paul Farley, *The Dark Film*, Picador, £12.99, ISBN 9781447212553
Tom Paulin, *Love's Bonfire*, Faber, £12.99, ISBN 9780571271535

Paul Farley's fourth collection opens with a poem in the imperative mood. 'The Power' has the dialectical structure of a sonnet, nine and a half lines of description separated by a caesura from an extended metaphor of eight and a half lines that switches from a seaside town to possibly the poet in his garret, invested with the power out of which Stephen King made a novel in *Fireraiser*, an expression of demonic possession or barely disguised feelings of neurotic omnipotence. The poem is typical in combining brilliance of imagery with an ability to build a poem around long sentences. Yet there are instances of sloppy writing. "Picture a seaside town / in your head" is an example of gratuitous padding to keep line lengths approximately the same. Where else are we conventionally to "picture" something? In our knees?

Farley creates a fragmented world, often based on childhood and adolescence, stock themes of the British mainstream. The cleverness of the poems makes them stand out with details from a northern childhood, "how real life was lived then: rain and spittle / ashes, cat's piss, crushed umbellifers...", woven into a spiral of association that can take a poem a long way from its starting point. 'Quality Street' is a fantasia travelling from the eponymous chocolate brand through history to myth and finishing not with "a strawberry cream" but with "Quinoline Yellow, Beta-carotene, / Allura red, Riboflavin, Tartazine", food dyes with dangerous side effects.

Later poems are less focused round childhood and some are distinctly unsatisfactory. 'Nostalgie Concrète's protagonist living backwards through time was done rather more powerfully in the novel *Time's Arrow* by Martin Amis. 'The Queen' seems to be a live performance piece falling short of too much disrespect but concluding with a brattish joke. The last verse begins "Imagine waking up" and concludes "realising, Jesus, I'm the fucking Queen!" This, however, is not as objectionable, as 'Boxer', which begins as an elegy to his dog, but whose sentimentality Farley has to disrupt with "the hole I dug / was so small, I had to break her leg / with the spade". The rest of us would have dug a bigger hole and dropped in her favourite toy. If Farley really wanted to be controversial he should have made the dog a Corgi.

Tom Paulin also seems to require a whiff of the bad boy. In the very first poem of *Love's Bonfire*, a badger comes to grief under his car and the callousness of making this a mere incident on the journey, "(couldn't – didn't – stop)", makes it part of an atmosphere where I assume that the personal and the public or political are supposed to interact or, in the case of this poem, fail to interact. Paulin's strategy in the opening and final thirds of the collection is to string together observations from the present with recollections of the past. The improvisatory style of the poems, with almost as many dashes as Emily Dickinson, leans towards Frank O'Hara. However, O'Hara had the gift of reducing his personality to a transparency through which the world strolled unalloyed by moral worry. In Paulin's poems we are always aware of a Protestant conscience nagging away at its place in the world. The Victorian cat is let out of the bag in the title poem with a quotation of Virgil's famous phrase "veteris vestigia flammae", which was the epigraph to Thomas Hardy's remorseful elegies for his first wife. Paulin is a Hardy scholar and his poems are satires of circumstance, the best of which is 'Sans Souci Park', where history and the present blend together in a virtuoso single-sentence stream of consciousness concluding with "with some cargo / braving the tide bar / like that ship in a bottle / or your too tired face / there at the window".

The central section provides the most powerful poems, translations of, or "poems after", Walid Khazendar, a Palestinian poet. The poems are engaged by the ever-present political deprivation of the Palestinians, but are all of a piece with Paulin's combination of personal detail and a larger social reality, as in 'A Single Weather', where a conversation takes place by a well that Palestinians can no longer use: "I could hear you trapped in your own voice / as we made sleaked talk – worse and worse – / by a well that since we were kids / no one'd drawn a bucket from ever". It's a pity that much of the rest of collection lacks such directness.

James Sutherland-Smith is a poet, translator, critic and lyric writer: selections of the Serbian poets Ivana Milankova and Miodrag Pavlovic will be published respectively by Arc and Salt.

"Gut strong – bone strong"

IAN BRINTON

Anthony Barnett, *Poems &,* Tears in the Fence/Allardyce Book ABP,
£48, ISBN 9780907954460
Anthony Barnett, *Translations,* Tears in the Fence/Allardyce Book ABP,
£36, ISBN 9780907954477

As poet and publisher for the past forty-five years Anthony Barnett has ploughed a solitary furrow, unerringly straight and hauntingly evocative across the field of English poetry. That furrow owes little to a notion of landscape or cityscape as it is conceived within the confines of much British poetry over the last half-century and, as Professor David Trotter pointed out in a review of Barnett's work in 1978, "Both as editor and poet, Anthony Barnett has always stood on the side of the island which faces the Continent. He is one of the few contemporary English writers to have learnt from a European tradition – in particular from the work of Paul Celan and Edmond Jabès." This sense of looking outward was evident from Barnett's early magazine, *Nothing Doing in London*, No. 1 1966 and No. 2 1968, in which the list of contributors ranged from Samuel Beckett to Edmond Jabès and from Andrew Crozier to George Oppen. However, as was also clear from the twenty-one issues of his mimeographed magazine, *The Literary Supplement*, his focus of interest was also firmly on the "Cambridge School" poets, and it was perhaps the bringing of these two areas together that prompted him to publish the first collected edition of the poems of J.H. Prynne in 1982 in a format that had more visual links with Gallimard than with any English publisher.

A similar concentration of focus is evident from the first glance at this new volume of collected poems with its ivory card cover and printed title in red, its substantial presence of nearly 700 pages and its intelligent awareness of the need for large spaces of white: silence out of which the printed word can speak with clarity and purpose. And, as can be seen from the inclusion of the ampersand in the book's title, the volume contains not only the sum of Anthony Barnett's poetry but also a range of fascinating prose-poems including 'Etiquette in the City' with its reference to the 'Radiant Garden', an image to which I shall return in a moment. It was in an interview with D.S. Marriott in 1992 that Barnett made his point clear about this need for space:

> The trumpet player Leo Smith, with whom I had the good fortune to work briefly, developed an important, yet, when you think about it, self-evident, theory of musical phrasing: what you play acts upon the silence, determines the nature, the sound of the silence which follows – and the silence, the music of the silence (not only other sound heard during the apparent silence) acts equally upon what you play, the phrase you previously played and the one with which you will follow the silence.

This sense of clarity and space was noticed by the Cambridge poet J.H. Prynne in his early readings of *A marriage* and the book-length *Poem About Music* published by Burning Deck in 1971. Writing to Barnett he declared that "You have the word lodged in the ear's labyrinth like a little pebble within that delicate fluid, otolith which sways to the sound passing over it", and, six years later, Prynne went on to refer to the words in the Ferry Press volume *Fear and Misadventure/Mud Settles* as being "completely innocent of habitual tonalities – those marks of a selfhood which reduce to social convention the aliveness of the reader". A typical short poem from that 1977 volume bears no title:

> With all the care in the world
> I feel things draw to a close
> though they are really far away.
>
> If they were around us.
>
> Where does this language
> *really* come from?
>
> A wise man would seek it
> close to home.

This pared-down language questions its own validity for dealing with suffering, and Barnett's own comments upon the writing of poetry seem entirely appropriate here:

> The poem is like the child born of the mother and the father but which is not them. It experiences the world. The child does not completely forget its origins, under any circumstances, ties are rarely completely severed, but the closer the poem remains to

home the more difficult it is for it to stand on its own feet, for it to be freed or to free itself and go out into the world.

The "wise man" may seek his language "close to home" but the poet's composition casts the message into a bottle with only the potential to be read by people other than the poet. That journey from the self to the other is what makes Heidegger suggest, in response to his own question 'Why Poets?', that poets "sense the track of the fugitive gods", and Anthony Barnett concludes his interview with Marriott by stressing that the poet's view has to be into a "radiant garden and all that implies".

Anthony Barnett remains one of the most important translators of poetry into English that we have in this country and in his lecture at Meiji University in 2002, titled 'Inexperience and Uncommon Sense in Translation', we can see why that should be. Taking as a starting point the well-worn notion that one can translate a poem but not the poetry of the poem, Barnett quotes Yves Bonnefoy turning this idea upside down. The contemporary French poet proposes that poetry, "the very thing we cannot grasp or hold", is the very thing we can translate, because, unlike the fixed nature of the poem itself, the poetry is unfixed. Bonnefoy says "You must realise that the poem, unlike poetry, is nothing and that translation is possible – which is not to say that it's easy; it is merely poetry re-begun." Barnett's collected *Translations* contains, amongst much else, work by the Japanese Akutagawa and the Italians Ungaretti and Zanzotto, whom Barnett sees as one of the most important European poets of our times, the German Celan, the Nordics Lagerkvist and Vesaas, and the French Giroux whose 1990 'Le Poème invisible' becomes *Blank* and opens:

> The Poem is this place where nothingness comes to see, comes to breathe.

Ian Brinton is Reviews Editor for *Tears in the Fence* and his most recent publication is *An Andrew Crozier Reader* (Carcanet); he is currently editing an edition of Crozier's prose for Shearsman.

Standing Poem Reclining

THOMAS A. CLARK

Ian Hamilton Finlay, *Selections,* University of California Press, £16.95, ISBN 9780520270596

For some years now, Ian Hamilton Finlay's fame as a gardener, sculptor or artist has overshadowed his reputation as a poet. Although Finlay himself insisted that all his activities were within the art of poetry, other poets have seemed particularly keen to evade the formal challenges of his work by assigning him to another category altogether. Part of the problem has been the absence of a substantial body of poetry in one volume, something you can take down from a shelf and read.

This lack would now seem to be filled with the publication of *Selections*, published by University of California Press as part of their Poets for the Millennium series and carefully edited by the poet's son Alec Finlay. It is a generous selection indeed, containing the bulk of Finlay's work that is publishable on a page. It is necessary to make this last qualification because the book contains few illustrations, none of them in colour. While this would hardly matter for almost any other poet, in Finlay's case it is a serious deprivation, undermining and warping the overall view of the work which the volume otherwise manages well.

A section of *Early Writings* includes one short story and one play before we find *The Dancers Inherit The Party*, first published by Migrant Press in 1960. This is the collection that was so warmly received by American poets such as Louis Zukofsky and Robert Creeley. Lorine Niedecker declared that the poems "simply set me free". Their plain diction, traditional rhymes, homely themes and folk-song clarity are a form of pastoral, deliberately removed from the density and sonority of mid-century modernist verse. A set of visual motifs, in metaphors of shape and colour, drifts away from a lyricism of place in search of the more objective poetics of concrete poetry.

The early 1960s brought a crisis: "'concrete' began for me with the extraordinary (since wholly unexpected) sense that the syntax I had been using, the movement of language in me, at a physical level was no longer there..." Concrete poems form the still centre of this book, Finlay's early and later writings falling away into conventional lineation on either side of them. With the *First Suprematist Standing Poem* (1965) a small discovery is made which will bring ruin to any attempt to adequately represent Finlay's main achievement in a volume such as this.

how blue ?   how blue !
how sad ?   how far !
how small ? how sad !
how white ? how small !
how far ?   how white !

Essentially a poem about the difference between two tones of voice, between a question mark and an exclamation mark, this was first published by Wild Hawthorn Press as a card. The main problem with it in *Selections* is simply that it does not *stand*. If a folded card can stand on its own, with the words up front, then poetry is taken off the shelf. The poem has moved from private into public space. The reader (or viewer) is *addressed*. This modest innovation had large consequences for Finlay, leading from many varied cards, posters, and gallery installations, to the famous garden at Little Sparta.

A similar problem occurs with the poem 'Cythera', given half a page in *Selections*:

air
in blue
leaf

blue bark
and blue leaf

a leaf
a barque
a blue leaf

a barque in leaf-blue
aire

In the original Wild Hawthorn Press edition, this delicate poem takes up a whole book; there are only a few words to a page, the turning of the pages gives the pace of the poem while revealing new aspects of sound and sense. We embark on a little voyage through the book.

The important early *canal stripe* and *ocean stripe* series in a similar way exploited the spatial and sequential possibilities of turning pages within one small book. They are not reproducible in another format. In later books, a play of words and images might open up areas of suggestion while building an ambience, friendly or fierce. They are often not reducible to the words alone, in conventional layout.

Selections has the laudable aim of presenting Ian Hamilton Finlay as a poet for the millennium. We might entirely agree, but his achievement is of a different order from the large, loose structures of poets in the Poundian tradition. Welcome as this volume is, it should be used with caution. Anyone wishing to understand the formal implications of Finlay's work, of how meaning and nuance may be developed through presentation, must seek out the small, rare editions from Finlay's own Wild Hawthorn Press.

Thomas A. Clark's latest book is *The Hundred Thousand Places* (Carcanet, 2009).

Elsewhere

WILL STONE

Yves Bonnefoy, *The Arrière-pays*, trans. Stephen Romer, Seagull Books, $25, ISBN 9780857420268

The *Arrière-pays* by celebrated French poet Yves Bonnefoy bears all the hallmarks of a quietly gathering miracle. It has been a long time coming, into English that is, but like all sacred objects that are the result of fateful trajectories, *The Arrière-pays*, whose eventful and prolonged passage to the UK was heroically navigated by the poet Stephen Romer, fell suddenly into the right hands, namely Seagull books, who have created an edition that through the eloquent community of its materials signals a respect and dedication to the text that most books today can barely muster. Romer's meticulous English translation reads with an unconscious resistance to forcedness most translators barely achieve.

The title itself, meaning roughly 'The Hinterland' or 'The Back Country', has no plausible equivalent in English and hence Romer wisely opted for retaining the French title. *L'Arrière-pays* was first published in 1972 by Swiss art publisher Skira. In the preface Bonnefoy expresses his concerns for an Anglicised version of the work, for its precise nature could not easily be delineated let alone categorised. Furthermore, images of mostly Italian art, churches and landscapes with captions (that somehow remind of Goya's extempore labels affixed to his etchings) were loosely interspersed with the text, recalling a French tradition that commenced with Belgian poet Georges Rodenbach's symbolist novel *Bruges-la-Morte* (1892) and was later employed by Surrealist chief André Breton for his *Nadja* (1928). Additional texts include 'The Place of Grasses', an engaging supplement to the original essay, and 'My Memories of Armenia', which opens with the intriguing "Our memories do not always convey the impression that they have some relation with our past..." and focuses on period photographs of ancient Armenian churches starkly positioned in landscapes of awe-inspiring solitude. The unadorned tone of these black-and-white images, the author argues, gives rise to a "cosa mentale", or an experience of the mind where the metaphysical aspiration may flourish. Echoes of the writer W.G. Sebald's preoccupations with time, landscape, history, the photographic image and oblivion are eerily present throughout *The Arrière-pays*, but perhaps no more pertinently than in this existentially succulent essay.

The Arrière-pays is a sometimes tortuous, always self doubting search for "presence" in the form of a lost domain, an "over there" or an "elsewhere", a realm which endowed ancient epochs with more manifest consciousness but which has now receded to the corner of our vision. "It is as if from the forces of life, from the syntax of colours and forms, from dense or iridescent words that nature perennially repeats, there is a single articulation we cannot grasp, even though it is one of the simplest; and our shining sun seems a blackness. Why can we not dominate what is there, like looking out from a terrace?" The crossroads, real or figurative, is the point at which the poet senses the path not taken, which might lead to this zone. The wayfarer traverses the lonely Tuscan and Umbrian plains wrestling with the notion of perspective or musing on the fragment of a medieval fresco being the X that marks the spot. In exploring this expanse of promising vistas and graciously accepted dead ends, he is assisted by a crew of poet forebears, namely Mallarmé and Yeats as representatives of the opposing positions within his own mind, while Rimbaud and Baudelaire intermittently whisper prophetically to the persevering traveller. Beyond the trials of the quest, the reader is treated to a series of visions culled from childhood reminiscences that seem to sway luxuriantly through the text like ripened corn. "It seemed to me Latin was like a thick dark green foliage, a laurel of the spirit through which I could make out a clearing, or at least the smoke from a fire, the sound of voices, a quivering of red cloth..."

Will Stone's latest collection is *Drawing in Ash* (Salt Publishing, 2011). His first English translation of an essay by Rilke's French translator Maurice Betz, *Rilke in Paris*, was published by Hesperus Press in July 2012.

The Word on the Street
Parnassus and Tin Pan Alley

The Poetry Society Annual Lecture

PAUL MULDOON

One of the several daunting aspects of the Poetry Society Annual Lecture is that the lecturer is required to include previously unpublished poems and to comment upon them, incisively and, I expect, insightfully. It would be hard enough to do this once. But twice? In London and Ledbury, on successive days! The way I've overcome that difficulty is by giving pretty much the same lecture on both occasions. I hope you're impressed by that solution. Coming up with unpublished poems is difficult, so I've decided to augment the few new poems I have with a few new song lyrics, and then to muse on the rather mysterious business of why poems become poems and songs songs. I'll also be trying to think through why I'm interested in trying to pursue both. I'm not going to be making any pronouncements on the subject. No position statement. I'm planning only to allow a few trends and tendencies to emerge.

The first thing I might say is that we tend to think of poetry writing and song-writing as being somewhat alike yet substantially unalike. In the way that, while they share a medium – water – Olympic springboard diving is somewhat like, yet substantially unlike, Olympic synchronised swimming. Or, in another season, luge and slalom. I cite these last examples partly because I notice that Mount Parnassus, once Muse central, is now home to two major Greek ski centres. Parnassus was where Apollo presented Orpheus with the lyre, on which he accompanied himself in his poem-songs. The culture I come from – the Irish – is a culture in which there's virtually no difference between poetry and song, between Parnassus and Tin Pan Alley. The term "Tin Pan Alley" is still applied to the area around Denmark Street in London and, in New York, to West 28th Street between Fifth and Sixth Avenues. This last was base camp for the likes of Irving Berlin, George and Ira Gershwin, and Cole Porter. There was certainly no sense of Parnassus being more important than Tin Pan Alley in the Ireland in which I was brought up. Our own house (called Annaya, of course, after a monastery near Beirut) was a house in which neighbours would drop in to sing or recite as the spirit moved them. It might be a Belfast street rhyme:

My Aunt Jane she brought me in
She made me tea out of her wee tin
Half a bap with sugar on the top
And three black balls out of her wee shop

Or it might be:

I wish I was on yonder hill
'Tis there I'd sit and cry my fill
And every tear would turn a mill
Is go dté tú mo mhuirnín slán
    Siúil, siúil, siúil a rúin
Siúil go socair agus siúil go ciúin
Siúil go doras agus éalaigh liom
Is go dté tú mo mhúirnín slán

We recognise the word "rune" in there. It's both the Irish and the English word for "secret". It may refer to a magical charm or spell. According to the *OED*, it may also refer to "any song, poem, or verse". There's a magical aspect to the incantatory element of both poems and songs. This may be partly because so many rely so heavily on repetition, not only in vocabulary but in the virtually mathematical replication of a stanzaic pattern:

I wish, I wish, I wish in vain
I wish I had my heart again
And vainly think I'd not complain
Is go dté tú mo mhúirnín slán

"And may you go safely, my darling" is the meaning of that refrain, by the way. We hear it in the Hiberno-English term "Mavourneen", just one of the Irish endearments like "Acushla" and "Alana" that have made it into English:

But now my love has gone to France
To try his fortune to advance
If he e'er comes back 'tis but a chance
Is go dté tú mo mhúirnín slán

This macaronic mishmash of languages is often associated with nonsense verse but it may also be found in a rather serious poem from my native county Armagh. This is *Aisling Airt Mhic Cubhthaigh*, 'The Vision

Journey of Art McCooey', a poet who lived between 1715 and 1773. The *aisling* is actually a form of political poem in which the poet is visited in a dream by a *speirbhean*, or "sky woman", whom he questions as to her identity, often showing off his magnificent grasp of Classical learning. He might enquire, for example:

> Are you Aurora or the goddess Flora,
> Artimedora or Venus bright,
> Or Helen fair beyond compare
> Whom Priam stole from the Grecian sight?

The woman is none of these, of course, but Ireland herself, a woman who's been shabbily treated by the man in her life, England. Like very few poems, but many songs, this one tends to have a point that it's going to make:

> *Ta mo chroise reabtha 'na mhile cead cuid*
> *'s gan balsam fein ann a d'foirfeadh dom phian*
> *Nuar a chluinim an Ghaelige uilig a teigbheail*
> *Is caismirt Bhearla I mbeol gach aoin;*
> *Bhullaidh is Jane ag glacadh leagsai*
> *Ar dhuichibh Eireann na mor-bhall caoin*
> *Is nuair fiafraim sceala, 's e freagra gheibhim:*
> 'You are a Papist, I know not thee.'

The first piece I'll share with you just happens to be a macaronic verse or two I've been trying to write for a musical project written by Dan Trueman, one of the founders of the Princeton Laptop Orchestra and a virtusoso on the Norwegian Hardangar fiddle. We're pretty sure it's going to be premiered by the Kronos Quartet and will feature the great Irish *sean nos* ("old style") singer, Iarla O' Lionaird. I'm not sure if all these verses will make it into the final version but it'll give you a sense of what parts of it might be like:

> One night Medhbh had brought me in
> *Ar scath a cheile a mhaireas na daoine*
> And made me tea out of her wee tin
> While she drank vodka martinis
> Then like a *speirbhean* had flown
> *Ochon agus ochon o*

Medhbh's singleminded double speak
Was no less a distortion
Than when Mick Machination and Brian O'Blique
Vied for the champion's portion
They hammed it up on the hambone
Ochon agus ochon o

Though she claimed to be on lemonade
Medhbh had seemed a little tiddly
When she came back from the cattle raid
She'd christened Tain Bo Diddley
She was in meltdown on methadone
Ochon agus ochon o

And it was still all fun and games
With O'Blique and Machination
Though they'd pencilled in their names
In the book of lamentations
Long before they were set in stone
Ochon agus ochon o

They talked from both sides of their mouths
They talked so much baloney
Ta si go measartha ta si go maith
Said O'Paque and Macaroni
Till the methadone clinic was on the phone
Ochon agus ochon o

Now day has wiped the floor with night
Day slumps in a neutral corner
The coffin-lid is screwed down tight
And our semi-professional mourners
Start their semi-professional moan
Ochon agus ochon o

You'll notice a little play on the name Muldoon there in the word "meltdown". The genre of the *aisling*, to which I also allude via the *speirbhean*, has its roots in the convention of the dream allegory we know from an author who's associated with the area in and around Ledbury, William Langland, also a punster on his own name in *The Vision of Piers Plowman*.

The phrase "Tain Bo Diddley" is a play on the name of one of the inventors of rock'n'roll, of course, combined with the title of the great Irish epic *Tain Bo Cuailgne*, much of which is set in County Armagh. My first attempt at a poem comes from a series based on a recent round-the-world voyage I made with the Institute for Shipboard Education. The working title of this series is '36 Views of Slieve Gullion' (Slieve Gullion being the major peak in South Armagh). As it happens, this poem is set in the Caribbean:

> Between Dominica and Martinique
> we go in search of sperm whales, listening for their tink-tink-tink
> on a hydrophone
> hooked up to a mini-speaker. A prisoner's tap
> on a heating pipe…
> The one faint hope by which he's driven.
>
> My son is reading *Lord of the Flies*. I can think of that book
> only as the dog-eared manuscript Charles Monteith would pick
> out of the slush pile at Faber's.
> I'm pretty sure dear Charles recognised
> a version of himself in Piggy. The same prep school anguish.
> Same avuncularity. Same avoirdupois.
>
> Now I imagine lying by my dead wife
> just as a sperm whale lies by its dead mate as if
> it might truly be said to mourn.
> A corruption of the Tamil term for "two logs
> lashed together with rope or the like,"
> the word we use is *catamaran*.

Now, it's pretty clear that poem's a poem and was never meant to be a song. Even Warren Zevon, who prided himself on having worked the word "brucellosis" into a song, would balk at trying to sing about "avuncularity" and "avoirdupois". The material is just too dense, and necessarily so. The song lyric is designed to be heard once and understood almost immediately. The pressure per square inch tends to be a lot less than it is in most poems. As we've heard more than once, for it's been true more than once, the poem brings its own music while the song needs music to become what it was destined to be. Like most writers, I suspect, I am struck day in day out by phrases or images (or combinations of the two), that might be components in a poem or song. It might be the idea that whales are no less capable of mourning than some of those "semi-professional" keeners in the macaronic song. It might be a line like "now day has wiped the floor with night". It might be a rhyme like "blossom / plasma" that's somehow tied in with an image of Saint Charbel and that monastery at Annaya after which our house was named. It might be a line like "You say you're just hanging out (but I know you're just hanging in)". It might be the phrase "Epistles at Dawn". One of the reasons I got involved in writing songs was, quite frankly, to avoid the compulsion to take every seemingly bright idea that came into my head and make a poem of it. This was a way in which I could lighten up and write what might be though of as the poetic equivalents of Graham Greene's entertainments. This one's called 'M.D. Boogie' and it's a riff on a series of medical doctors:

> Watson had lived on Baker Street
> At 221b
> When he married Miss Mary Morstan
> He sublet his rooms to me
> When he married that Mary Morstan
> He sublet his rooms to me
> Jung's notion of the archetype
> He shared with the Navaho
> As for the collective unconscious
> He kinda went with the flow
> As for the collective unconscious
> Jung kinda went with the flow
>
> Dr Pepper hails from Waco
> Along with our friend Steve
> We're such typical Americans
> We're so ill-prepared to grieve
> We're such typical Americans
> We've no idea how to grieve
> I always liked Dr Feelgood
> But King Crimson had soul
> Neither of those bands will get to play
> Half time at the superbowl
> Neither will have wardrobe malfunctions
> Half time at the superbowl

Things are going fairly well up until this point. Let's face it, though, a choice has to be made. Are we going to continue in this vein forever, as we might in the interminable ballad structure of AAAAAA, or are we going to mix things up a bit? What about AAB? It's from that impulse not to bore that the middle eight, or bridge, stems:

> Holliday would make no house calls
> Unless to Marshall Earp
> Or somebody like that
> You keep coming around with pancakes
> You want to borrow some syrup
> Or something like that

My hunch is that the sestet of the Italian sonnet derives from this same impulse to introduce a fresh idea, often one that's set at an angle to the octave. In the case of this song lyric, we leave AAB and return to A:

> That medical marijuana
> They sold on Venice Beach
> You came to a realisation
> It was way out of reach
> You came to a realisation
> It was way way out of reach
> Stanley was sent by the *Herald*
> In search of Livingstone
> You've been asking me incessantly
> Why I won't throw you a bone
> You've been asking me incessantly
> Why I won't throw you a bone

Let me now turn to Elizabeth Barrett (Elizabeth Barrett Browning as she would become). This is from the Preface to 'The Battle of Marathon', written in 1819 and published in 1820: "In my opinion, humble as it is, the custom of riming would ere now have been abolished amongst poets, had not Pope, the disciple of the immortal Dryden, awakened the lyre to music, and prove that rime could equal blank verse in simplicity and gracefulness, and vie with it elegance of composition, and in sonorous melody. No one who has read his translation of Homer, can refuse him the immortality which he merits so well, and for which he labored so long. He it was who planted rime for ever in the regions of Parnassus, and uniting elegance with strength, and sublimity with beauty, raised the English language to the highest excellence of smoothness and purity."

The fact that Elizabeth Barrett was a mere fourteen-year-old when she wrote 'The Battle of Marathon' should hardly be held against her, though it may explain her tendency to show off in the "Are you Aurora / Or the goddess Flora?" vein. "Paphia's Queen," for example, is Aphrodite:

> And still from smoking Troy's once sacred wall,
> Does Priam's reeking shade for vengeance call,
> Minerva saw, and Paphia's Queen defied,
> A boon she begored, nor Jove the boon denied:
> That Greece should rise, triumphant o'er her foe
> Disarm th' invaders, and their power o'erthrow.

This ambition to tell a story is one that's not particularly to the fore in modern poetry, but it continues to be a vital element of almost all songs, even those that look more like 500-metre dashes than marathons. On the subject of marathons, I was intrigued by this piece in *The Economist* of June 2: "It has been a tricky task for Kenya's athletics authorities to choose a three man team for the coming Olympic marathon... The 20 fastest men's times over the 26.2 miles in the past year have all been run by Kenyans... Even the world-record holder, Patrick Makau, has failed to get a place in the Olympic team... The Kenyans' history of marathon glory has its sad side. Samuel Wanjiru, the reigning Olympic champion, will not be defending his title because he died in a fall from a balcony last year. An investigation into his death revealed a precociously gifted athlete with an apparently insatiable appetite for women, alcohol and guns."

As someone with an appetite for at least two out of those three, I find that report quite heartening. Much as I'm interested in going the longer distance, I suspect I'm less a marathon runner than a 100-metre hurdler, more likely to attempt the kind of patter song with a tongue-twisting text we recognise in everything from Gilbert and Sullivan's 'I am the very model of a modern Major-General' through Warren Zevon's 'Werewolves of London' with its "A little old lady got mutilated late last night" to Elvis Costello's 'Pump It Up'. Only rarely nowadays does poetry seem to include the exhortation to "pump it up", but erotics are a major staple of the popular song. I love that description of the difference between country music and rock'n'roll, country being driven by extramarital sex and drink, rock'n'roll by premarital sex and drugs. Here's a little ditty entitled 'The Adult Thing', which will be included in *Songs and Sonnets*, a collection due a little later this year from Enitharmon:

It was obvious Newt and Rudy
Were having an affair
JFK was doing Judy
While Jackie did her hair
Since LBJ and FDR
Opened up the West Wing
The guy at the end of a bar
Has pocketed his ring
And done the adult thing
The adult thing
He's done the adult thing

Since Tarzan cheated with Cheetah
And Monica with Bill
The Master with Margarita
In Margaritaville
Since Prince Charles and Princess Di
Were clearly born to swing
And Henry VIII came to vie
With Martin Luther King
I've done the adult thing
The adult thing
I've done the adult thing

Now I view the world through a salted rim
Since I found out about your night with Jim
And I'm starting to wonder if it's true
Adultery's the adult thing to do

You could see Kobe and Magic
Needed more triple sec
While Nelson lay hemorrhagic
On the *Victory*'s deck
At least Einstein would never ask
"How long's a piece of string?"
At least Einstein would never mask
His having had a fling
He did the adult thing
The adult thing
He did the adult thing

That "hemorrhagic" is another nod in the direction of the brucellosis-flaunting Warren Zevon, as is the "Jim," a direct allusion to the line "He'll rip your your lungs out, Jim" from 'Werewolves of London'. Or, as I now call it, 'Werewolves of London and Ledbury'. Now, no music has been written for 'The Adult Thing'. One thing is sure, though. Because of its structure, music may be written for it. And music of almost any stripe. It could be a mid-tempo country song. It could be a headlong rock song. It could be a heartwarming, if slightly ironised, ballad. The point is that, in this case, the words come before the music. I was encouraged to hear P.J. Harvey tell the *New Musical Express* in 2011: "My writing's changed quite a lot over the last four or five years. I work on words entirely separately from music and spend a lot of time making a word-form work on the page... I found that it does actually strengthen my songs, if they become songs, because it has to work at that root level."

There are songwriters like Paul Simon who, astonishingly for someone whose words are so brilliant, insists on writing the music first on the principle that if the music isn't catchy it really doesn't matter how good the lyric might be. On balance, though, the level of lyric writing would benefit from a slightly more rigorous approach. This is not to say that a sense of a performer's musical style mightn't influence the style of a song. Here's a piece that is, at the moment, part of '36 Views of Slieve Gullion'. It was written for a Ghanian *griot* called Sherrif Ghale who joined our recent Semester at Sea voyage in Brazil and crossed the Atlantic with us to his homeland. As you may recall, a *griot* is a West African bard who combines the roles of "historian, story teller, praise singer, poet and musician". The two elements that came together to cause a chemical reaction were the sight of my wife braiding her hair and the fact that there's an extraordinary "meeting of the waters" of the Rio Negro and the Amazon near the city of Manaus. You may remember the character of Fitzcarraldo, played by Klaus Kinski, stumbling late into the Manaus opera house at the start of Werner Herzog's great film:

> Because they flow at different speeds
> and different temperatures
> two rivers may lie side by side
> and never be a pair.
> One river sets its pewter
> by another's earthenware...
> It takes time for darker water
> to blend in with the fair.
> *These things would come together where*
> *I watched a woman braid her hair.*

Not since Edgardo stabbed himself
at the end of *Lammermoor*
has the Manaus opera house
seen such wear and tear.
Not since the rubber barons
have we heard so much hot air
about keeping up appearances.
Now we're forced to repair

to the Teatro Amazonas
where Italian marble-masons
paved the way
for Patti and Pavarotti
to play characters whose bravado
had them say:
"These things would come together where
I watched a woman braid her hair."

The "Patti" I'm referring to in the bridge isn't Patti Smith, by the way, but Adelina Patti (1843–1919), a singer who used to demand $5,000, in gold, before she came on stage. When I happened on this factoid, my first thought was "Does the Poetry Society know about this?"

Now vine-laden weaver-birds
swing from the chandeliers
and try the kind of somersault
very few will dare...
It takes time for darker water
to blend in with the fair
as when Scottish iron-workers
worked themselves into the stairs.
These things would come together where
I watched a woman braid her hair.

That image of the Scottish ironworkers who "worked themselves into the stairs" is a harking back to an opera I wrote about twenty years ago which featured some elements of the life and times of Frank Lloyd Wright and included the patter song line "It's the fate of every woodworker / To fade into his own woodwork". This next piece I'll read was written specifically for a composer whose best-known opera was also a biopic, given that its subject was Anna Nicole Smith. I've been working recently with Mark-Anthony Turnage, the composer of *Anna Nicole*, which premiered last year at the Royal Opera House, on a piece which was commissioned by the Honorable the Irish Society, the City of London and the Verbal Arts Centre in Derry, and which will be performed simultaneously next July 3rd in London and Londonderry (not Ledbury!) by the London Symphony Orchestra and Camerata Ireland. The subject of our choral piece is not Elizabeth Barrett's "smoking Troy's once sacred wall" but the still-sacred Walls of Derry. As is the case of a West African *griot*, this is a case of the poet taking the opportunity to write a public piece that combines history, story telling, and maybe even praise:

> It's only a stone's throw from here
> To where a gate being barred
> Would send a signal loud and clear
> A heart may be set hard
> May be... may be...
> A heart may be set hard
> *An doire* took its Gaelic name
> From a grove of oak trees
> So Derry's walls would stand
> For durability
> Dura... Dura...
> For durability
> Would stand for our resting assured
> Of being hemmed in... being immured
>
> *Doire*... the Druids... at their core
> The sacred oak... *an dair*
> The oak so stalwart it stands for
> All we've stood for thus far
> All we've... all we've...
> All we've stood for thus far
> We're proud to live under duress
> Our ranks are so steadfast
> But such endurance must mean less
> When only rancours last
> Only... only...
> When only rancours last
> For only rancours rest assured
> Of being hemmed in... being immured

We shut ourselves within a six feet thick wall
That will withstand both cannonball
And being undermined
And being undermined
And there we huddle
Through maelstrom and muddle
With a strong sense of being maligned
Of being maligned

You notice that little play on the name Muldoon in "maelstrom and muddle?" I'm sure you know I introduce that kind of thing mostly to relieve the tedium.

Some minor slight or disregard
Still has us come to blows
From here to where the gate was barred
Being merely a stone's throw
Merely... merely...
Being merely a stone's throw
We know that Derry's unsurpassed
In stoutly holding out
If we still need something to cast
Then let it be a doubt
Let it... let it...
Then let it be a doubt
That we might ever rest assured
Of being hemmed in... being immured

It's very refreshing to be able to work from time to time with such a large canvas. It's a bit like painting on a gable wall, using a broad stroke one usually associated with a political mural or a whitewash brush. Another thing I love about song-writing, in addition to the forthright sociological aspect whereby one may decently make points in public without becoming a propagandist, is its social aspect. Rather than sit alone day in day out, there's an opportunity to interact with talented composers and performers. I've just recently been writing a couple of songs with the Irish singer-songwriter, Paul Brady, of whom Bob Dylan once said "some guys have got it down – Leonard Cohen, Paul Brady, Lou Reed, secret heroes". This is a song Paul Brady and I are working on right now:

Like two characters
From Looney Toons
We've been mowing your lawn
Since early afternoon
Maybe the blades being clogged with grass
Or plain old running out of gas
Had the mower pack it in
Maybe it's a job with perks
But my patience for yard work
Is really wearing thin
So when I hear you say
We should have a little drink
I'm with you all the way
I like how you think
I like how you think

I've been listening with one ear
To the Caps versus the Bruins
I've been on a losing streak
Since mid-afternoon
Maybe your husband's little rule
About not opening the pool
Had me throw in the sponge
Maybe the fact he's out of town
Means you might still be down
For taking the plunge
And when I hear you say
You're hovering on the brink
I'm with you all the way
I like how you think
I like how you think

Sombody tell me please what's with the smell
Of a new mown lawn
The minute it hits my nose I'm thinking Don Juan

By way of preamble to the final verse, I should mention that I was more than a little taken aback when, a couple of years ago, I was sitting in a podiatrist's office and looked up to read the legend "April Is National Podiatry Month". Given that, in the US, April is designated as National Poetry Month, my first thought was, "Does the Poetry Society of America know about this?"

> National Podiatry Month
> Can't be over too soon
> Though we'll have walked ten miles
> Come late afternoon
> Maybe we'll get to fall asleep
> Where the cuttings are heaped
> And not wake until dawn
> Maybe we'll rewind the hose
> Once we've watered the one rose
> That blooms on your back lawn
> For when I hear you say
> You don't mind a little kink
> I'm with you all the way
> I like how you think
> I really like how you think

One of the benefits of attempting to write songs has been the carrying over of song structures into some recent poems. This is another section from '36 Views of Slieve Gullion' that's driven by a verse form that we find not only in the sestet of some sonnets but, as I mentioned earlier, in many popular songs:

> In the Slave Castle at Cape Coast
> I saw slaves pushed from pillar to whipping-post
> on their way out of Ghana
> by the Door of No Return.
> I suppose any plain-backed pipit might learn
> to sound the vox humana
>
> from its organ-reed, given how a woman may take wing
> above an open sewer and sing,
> making not only her own spirits quicken
> but gladdening the heart of a boy who trots in her wake.
> She glances back to where the boy (her son?) makes
> like that mangy chicken
>
> shooting its cuffs because its suit's so hot.
> It being noon, she hasn't much of a shot

at casting a shadow,
even though she carries home
a mess of fish in a basket set on a blue latex foam
mattress pad no

self-respecting fish would be seen dead on.
Near the Grace of God Nail Salon
she pauses to take the basket
from her head,
as though to ponder if she might choose, instead
of a fish-shaped casket,

a casket in the shape of a beer-bottle or speed boat.
The mangy chicken, plus a mangy goat,
chime in with the plain-backed pipit
to celebrate her setting the basket back atop
her head as she draws level with the Vote for Jesus Wig Shop.
If there's a balance now I'm inclined to tip it

in favor of the boy who comes back double quick
to seize my wrist despite its being slick
with sun tan lotion.
After his recent brush with mange
he, too, is able to rearrange
himself with almost as little commotion –

with almost as little to-do –
as the military coup
that ousted Kwame Nkrumah.
Now I see that his entire outfit, from his football shirt
to his sneakers shining in the dirt,
comes courtesy of Puma.

The rhyming of "shadow / pad no" and "pipit / tip it" is influenced by Boy George Michael Gordon, Lord Byron, who specialised in such effronteries. I was delighted to see that Leonard Cohen performs Byron's "We'll Go No More a-Roving" as a poem-song. The list of "stuff" in that poem set in Ghana reminds me of – may even be partly inspired by – the list of "stuff" in one of my very favourite poems:

Quinquireme of Nineveh from distant Ophir,
Rowing home to haven in sunny Palestine,
With a cargo of ivory,
And apes and peacocks,
Sandalwood, cedarwood, and sweet white wine.

The beauty of 'Cargoes' by John Masefield, another of the great poets of Ledbury, is that its finicky list-making is totally of a piece with the ambitions of the bill of lading. The contrast between the opulence of the items in the first verse is tellingly contrasted with the nitty-gritty of the last:

Dirty British coaster with a salt-caked smoke stack,
Butting through the Channel in the mad March days,
With a cargo of Tyne coal,
Road-rails, pig-lead,
Firewood, iron-ware, and cheap tin trays.

While one would never say that the poem can't take in everything and anything in its hold, I can't help but think that the song lyric may often be even more capacious, allowing for more by way of the "firewood, iron-ware and cheap tin trays" of various ragbag, rough and ready registers. Like many of the songs in *The Word on the Street*, a collection of rock lyrics published next February by Faber, this next one is performed by Wayside Shrines, the Princeton-based musical collective to which I belong:

The elephants have done a bunk
They've left on the late train
For when it comes to packing trunks
They're speedy in the main
And when it comes to skipping town
The elephants have got it down
To a fine art
They too refuse to act their age
And when they go on the rampage
They're off the chart
They still rely quite heavily on scent
For figuring out what it all meant

The elephants know project teams
Are good for rolling logs

You think I'm pushy and I seem
To treat people like cogs
Because push always comes to shove
The elephants go hand in glove
In single file
When the dust settled on our show
You had me thinking you might go
The extra mile
To where we'd find a spot to pitch our tent
And figure out what it all meant

The "drive-in" mentioned in the final verse is not a drive-in in the restaurant sense but in the movie theatre sense.

The elephants are less disposed
To hard work now they've found
The Vineland drive-in will stay closed
Until the spring comes round
The Vineland drive-in has two screens
Where everything we've ever seen
Was at a slant
The elephants take in both sides
As each projects on its own hide
An elephant
They also see how little time we've spent
In figuring out what it all meant

This next poem comes from *Songs and Sonnets*, the book published by Enitharmon. It's another section from the sequence '36 Views of Slieve Gullion' and it's simply an attempt to get down a giraffe. In this case, a giraffe at a water-hole. I was struck while watching giraffes in Zululand by the similarity of the patterns on their coats and the mirror image of cracked clay around their water-hole. The lorgnette in the first line is the "pair of eyeglasses mounted on a handle" through which one might have squinted on the opening night of *Anna Nicole*. The lorgnette is a way of extending the length of the giraffe's neck:

Though her lorgnette
and evening-gloves
suggest she's made for the role
of an opera-buff

singing along with the score,
her mouth's out of sync
with her own overdub.

A giraffe that flubbed
her lines coming back to drink
just a little more
of the bubbly stuff
from the dried-out mud hole
in which a reflection of
her upper body's already set.

Next is the title song from *The Word on the Street*, an everyday tale of addiction and things not adding up. The term "hunky-dory" is a very *sotto voce* shout-out to the great singer-song-writer Dory Previn, who died on February 14th of this year:

It's still the party line
The official position
Everything's still fine
At 17th and Mission
It's all still sweet
It's all hunky-dory
But the word on the street
That's another story
The word on the street
Is we're quitting
Now our course is run
The word on the street
Is you're splitting
The word on the street
Is we're done

When the news first broke
The conventional wisdom
Was they found no coke
In the cockatoo's system
All's still going a treat
We're just fine and dandy
But the word on the street

Is you're into nose candy
The word on the street
Is we've tasted
The scourings of the fleshpots
The word on the street
Is you're wasted
The word on the street
Is we're shot

The trooper must have stated that official position
When he pulled you over on Friday night
Even as he was charging you with possession
You insisted everything was shipshape despite

The rumours they might float
For the prevailing doctrine
Is still our little boat
Has a sturdy cockswain
All's trim and neat
We're just super-duper
But the word on the street
Is you tried to buy that trooper
The word on the street
Is no one's talking
Except maybe the cockatoo
It says the word on the street
Is you're walking
The word on the street
Is we're through

The poignancy of that last verse of 'The Word on the Street' is very, very difficult to manage in a poem. That's another very appealing aspect of trying to write songs – it affords the opportunity for the kind of emotional ramping-up that I hardly ever entertain in a poem.

I'll end with two pieces. The first is part of a poem set in Japan, one of our last ports of call on our recent Semester at Sea:

As a sumo wrestler enters the ring
the handful of salt he flings
is his grandmother's faint

shadow still somehow
flung on the pavement in Hiroshima.
Even then my mother's granite jaw was set
on a wound that never healed.

The body of Father Charbel exuded white and red
fluids long after he was dead.
My mother prayed till he was made a saint.
Sometimes a cherry tree will hold out its blossom
like a bag of plasma
held out from a bayonet
on a long abandoned battlefield.

And, finally, a song lyric that appears on a new CD by Brian Kennedy,
the Irish singer-songwriter. This is a song we wrote together for the Belfast
Nashville Country Music Festival of 2011. The imagery is drawn from Brian
Kennedy's own life as a child in Belfast, when he first learned to sing by trying
to get in tune with the night sounds of police cars, ambulances and fire engines.
I'm going to let it stand for the artist's attempt to be in sync with her or his
moment, sometimes as a springboard diver, sometimes a synchronised
swimmer:

In '68 and '69
The Belfast fire brigade would find
How petrol met its match
Through Lenadoon and Ligoniel
I'd hear an ambulance appeal
Its having been dispatched
In Ligoniel and Lenadoon
The bomb squad had been primed
But though the times were out of tune
Something would always chime
At six I thought it was in fire
Or blood I'd been baptised
For when I heard a siren wail
I'd try to harmonise
Yeah when I heard a siren wail
I'd try to harmonise

From Christopher and Bleecker Streets
I recognised that song so sweet
By which some men are bound
Almost as soon as I'd arrived
In old New York I hit the dives
Yet never ran aground
I sailed again almost as soon
For more familiar climes
Where though the times were out of tune
Something would always chime
Now music lured me on to rocks
Where I'd gladly capsize
And when I'd hear a siren wail
I'd try to harmonise
Yeah when I'd hear a siren wail
I'd try to harmonise

In Phoenix Park and Dolphin's barn
We'd spin ourselves a 3-ply yarn
That we were more than fit
To catch a tiger by the tail
The warning signs all said we'd fail
That we'd be biters bit
The warning signs still say we'll fail
Bogged down in deficit
But I hope Ireland's not immune
To turning on a dime
For though the times are out of tune
Something will always chime
I know how holding out some hope
Is seen as ill-advised
But when I hear a siren wail
I still try to harmonise
Yeah when I hear a siren wail
I still try to harmonise

Paul Muldoon, a former President of the Poetry Society, is the author of eleven full-length collections of poems.

℘

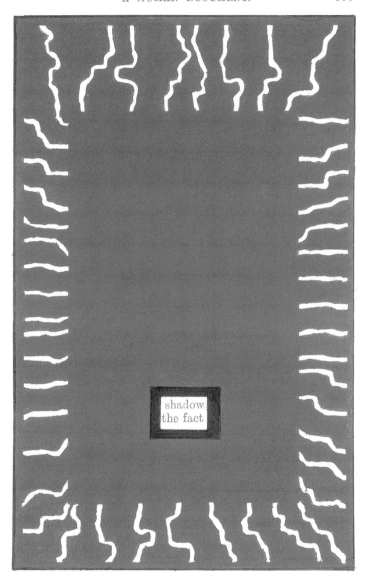

Declan Ryan
From Alun Lewis

There is nothing that can save today, darling,
you not being here. You MUST write.
It's impossible to breathe otherwise.
I'm only talking of the things I really NEED.
I'm so tired of travelling away from you.
I think of you all the bloody time. Do you mind?

This isn't an answer or a letter –
it's only a cup of coffee after lunch.
Many things I've been unable to remember
came to me last night.
You sitting like a babu at a desk
in the bowels of the G.P.O.
You standing in the quartier latin corridor
of the Hotel Marina on Sunday afternoon
after the cinema saying 'Alright, pay the taxi. Let's stay.'

When I saw you on Saturday July 24th
you were the flash of a sword.
Now I'm hopelessly shut into the camp life again.
A soccer match, a disjointed conversation at dinner,
a visit to the reading room to see how things go:
oh and a longing beyond words.

There's a fat dove strutting across the lawn
by the bougainvillea.
I wish I could be strolling with you
looking at the rose moles all in stipple
in your little stream.
One way or another I make a lot of shadows where I go.

Don't worry over the hairs on my head.
May you not be tried harder than you can bear.
Let there be an again, New Year. Save us.

Note: This poem uses material taken from Alun Lewis's letters to Freda Aykroyd,
collected in *A Cypress Walk* (Enitharmon, 2006).

Judy Kravis
His heroic youth

I looked at him in his heroic youth, busting with vitality, if chemical, eyes
tuned, plan b already in operation, one shoulder dropped a little. After
your death, I said, I'll get to know your daughter. This wasn't prescience. He
had already died and his daughter was there with me, watching. After his
death it was hers to play. The sadness and the confusion could be
contained, at her own risk. I understand why he loved you, she said.

James Sutherland-Smith
Nuptials

Two Silver-Washed Fritillaries over clumps of hairy-stemmed scabious;
the male, I assume from its larger size, darker spots and the green pattern
on the underside of its wings like a fragment of a large scale ordnance
survey map, is mostly inert when the female flies to another flowerhead,
as all females of the species so much more versatile than the male,
which hangs from her like a piece of delicate luggage although occasionally
he stirs and then the pair seem to be one large butterfly with slightly
       asymmetrical wings.

A third fritillary, another male, attempts to butt in and there is a brief orgy
of orange shot through with black and green over the pink scabious before
the mating pair ascend to continue and conclude on the leaves of a
       neighbouring hazel bush and the intruder glides off.

Later I find the first male spent on the grass by my cabin.

He does not fly away when I stoop over him.

Mona Arshi
Ghazal

Not even our eyes are our own...
  – *Frederico García Lorca,* The House of Bernarda Alba

I want to tune in to the surface, beside the mayfly,
listen to how she holds her decorum on the skin of the pond.

I want to sequester words, hold them in stress positions,
foreignate them, string them up to ripen on vines,

and I want to commune with rain and for the rain to be
merciful, a million tiny pressures on my flesh.

I refuse to return as either rose or tulip but wish
to be planted under the desiring night sky.

I want to be concentrated to a line under the pleat of your palm
and for it to radiate opalesque under shadow.

I want God's fingers to break and for you to watch as I
fold over my sleeve, reveal the detail of my paling wrist.

Andrew Elliott
The Milkman

Many things have come to pass which I will never understand,
not least among them my father who came from outer space
to find my mother in the corner of a field, milking the cow –
left to last – which had only to look over her shoulder to know
that her favourite milkmaid's mind was no match for a creature
which having travelled this far to hatch would be willing
to stand there for a few minutes more, allowing its shadow
to creep up her spine to where the sun has turned red in her hair

as I often suppose it must do in mine when one of those women –
who I like to leave until late in my round – opens her door,
still in her dressing gown, and tells me that there's something
that she'd like me to see. *Oh*, she'll say, *let me take those...*
leading the way to the kitchen at the back, a breezeblock extension,
where the kettle will be boiling on its little blue jet and I'll think
of my father, hurtling through space, delivering in good faith
the powers of which I am not short. *Here*, she'll say, *just baked.*

Robert Stein
Fourteen Untitled Images, 1919

When you first said your name I heard
Each letter crawl like an insect across my throat
And this morning I dreamt also the shadow of your arm thrown
Across my chest. Please stop.

The one with your head bagged in the net of your veil
I shall call by your initials and then 'Suffragette'.

Tuesday, can you call on me then? At ten in the evening? The darkness
    will be right.
Or the next day.
              Dear Miss Jasternová, your shadow has
Slipped under the door to visit me again.

Before falling in love with you, therefore, I would like to say
That you ought to know, for example
That of the thirty-eight photographs of you
Taken in my studio that evening,
None show all of you.
Sixteen show none of you at all.

I'm not making myself clear am I?
Good morning, Miss Jasternová, to start again,
On the spiral staircase where I photographed you twice yesterday,
Your hat I saw was a species of snail.

I prize snails. I also have already framed
The one of your head bagged in its black net, teeth tight and netted too.
I assure you it's quite in order to show me one breast
As I am looking the other way, as you can see, only
My camera slides and blinks away, opens and re-tightens again through
    the shadows.

In Zlín, anyway, it will not be seen as your breast.
A stone, the moon's mountain, no more. Don't go away.

I have fifteen portraits, all of them called 'Shadow'.
I notarise the grains of darkness.
I have photographed sleep.

This is the first shutter-camera in the Letná district.
I plan your legs, heavily shadowed,
As swept sand-bars, and your throat, ungulping, nude, two-bladed,
Is past any love we might feel.

Steel yourself, Miss Jasternová –
I shall have it all over Zlín. I mean to have the world out.

Candy Neubert
ways to leave

Couldn't imagine, ducking from the porch,
hurrying through the yard with the lantern,
finding the nail to hang it just inside
the barn door, all hay, muck, and animal,
saying some quiet words, running a hand
down her ready flank, sorting out the tack,
saddling up, familiar rub of leather
through fingers, slipping the halter, snuffing
the lamp, always with the same quiet words,
all right there good girl fine girl, never mind
a bit of rain tonight, we have to leave,
now off we go, and hooves sound on the lane,
this very lane where no one could conceive
these keys, ignition, headlights, radio.

Graham Allison
Leaving Buenos Aires

Walking around San Telmo
early in March, the heat has eased,
and the first heavy rain fallen.
I stop at the Walrus bookshop
on Estados Unidos and buy Jaume
Bukowski's *Women*. I go down
Defensa, through the crowds
hovering about street stalls;
some are already starting to pack up.
I stop for a beer in Plaza Dorrego,
then go back, shower and change.

I am the first to arrive at Desnivel.
Jaume turns up, Cinta is with him,
Uli couldn't make it. Nor could Eline.
I give Jaume Bukowski's *Women*.
Dan and Raffaella bring along two friends
of Raffaella's I haven't met before.
Amanda drags in her latest, a Frenchman.
Baleria and her girlfriend Andrea arrive.
We eat grilled cheese, slabs of steak,
beef sausages, tortilla espaňyola and salad.
Afterwards we go to a bar, drink
Quilmes Bokke, mess about with peanuts.
We don't stay too late, tomorrow
Dan and I leave for Puerto Madryn.

Naomi Foyle
from Witwalking

XIII

tell me where your childhood shrivelled on the cracked
earth coarse grass of your parents' neglected lawn were you
left too long in the sun no one careful to find you shade

Twenty years later a kid from Brooklyn made a film. *The Squid and the Whale.*
He'd had it rough. *Both* his parents were writers:
Dad a beached novelist, spouting off
to his hot female students; Mom wrapping her tentacles round rave reviews,
an ex-tennis pro, the pulpy hearts of her sons. The future director
apes his father's pretensions; his little brother jacks off in the library
smears fistfuls of sperm all over the books.
Divorced academics served up as an indie-flick squirm-fest.
In Cinema Four at the Camden Odeon, I indulged my love of projection –
Laura Linney's straight brown hair, Pink Floyd's *The Wall*,
teenage self-bondage: a banquet of light, made just for me.
I could have licked the screen.
Now I didn't have to write that nauseating novel:
A midwestern campus town. The eighties. Who slept with who,
when, where and why? Which kid walked in? Who took the dog? Who
blamed the feminist dean? Who couldn't cook? Who tried smoking dope?
Who remarried? Who shacked up? Who ordered every cocktail on the menu
and loudly sang the praises of the clit? Who forked out for tuition? Who
paid off my credit card? Who hummed Leonard Cohen's 'Joan of Arc'
when I shaved my head and dyed the stubble blonde? Who made me
wear a hat until my hair grew back?
Who never properly lived
with either one again? Who went to study in Toronto, shagged every last
cowpunk on Queen St, ate a Polish bakery, stuck her finger down her
throat? Who gained a stone anyway, came home for Christmas looking
pregnant? Whose 'home' was two new houses? Who devoured two
helpings of turkey and pudding, took the dog for a walk, vomited
into a hole in the snow?

> Who, in the end that is never The End,
> thought it was better both parents were 'happy'? Who swallowed
> the whole fucking prairie (dirt, nettles, thistles) stowed it for years
> in her bathysphere belly, disgorged it an ocean away?

tell me where...: from 'damage' in Brenda Riches, *Something to Madden the Moon* (Turnstone Press, 1991).

Liane Strauss
In the Divorce

my mother got my teeth and my hair and my
father got my eyes, which was funny
because everybody always told me I have my mother's.

Just like my friend Josh, my father got my weekends.
my crossword puzzles and my bike, and my mother got my sulks.
My father, my ingenuity; my mother, my no getting around it.

What my father didn't get, according to my mother,
was *everything*, or *anything*, depending on something
I never could work out. What my mother wouldn't stop until she got,
according to my father, was the last word, or his last red cent.

She also got my brother. My father got a girlfriend.
I got my father. My brother got a hamster.
My mother got a white sofa, finally rid of the leaky armchair
from the Salvation Army, or the teamsters, in Cleveland,
and I got one of those brand new oversized ersatz barnyard antique clocks.

Rosie Shepperd
"Don't take drugs, Allen, get married"

(The first response of Allen Ginsberg's mother to Howl*)*

My mother never tells me that the president plants listening
devices in our home, or that her ex-mother-in-law is poisoning
Prometheus (the cat) with polonium; she is just plain impossible
in her own way, just as I'm impossible in mine, and you too are impossible.

And OK, she says she's convinced she's being stalked by someone
at a call-centre in South East Asia and no, that's not much to go on
but I'm lucky I've never had to take trips with her on the cross-town
to see an Upper East-Side therapist with a mustard stain on his trousers.

And is she so out-of-touch that nothing she says means very much?
Not like us; when you speak, I listen and when I speak, you listen harder.
And does she hand out precise and less-than-well-meant advice?

"If you consider me in nothing, honey, consider me in this:
Poetry won't make you thin or rich, writing just makes you a reader.
Don't mix with people of prejudice and most especially the Dutch."

Hannah Lowe
Dance Class

The best girls posed like poodles at a show
and Betty Finch, in lemon gauze and wrinkles,
swept her wooden cane along the rows
to lock our knees in place and turn our ankles.
I was a scandal in that class, big-footed
giant in lycra, joker in my tap shoes,
slapping on the off-beat while a hundred
tappers hit the wood. I missed the cues
each time. After, in the foyer, dad,
a black man, stood among the Essex mothers
clad in leopard skin. He'd shake his keys
and scan the bloom of dancers where I hid
and whispered to another ballerina
he's the cab my mother sends for me.

Julia Reckless
Fly Away Home

Peonies drip on my ladybird buttons,
congeal in gauzy blue wool.
I am four, on the floor from a punch.
The black tarmac sticks in my turned-back palms,

I grit my teeth –
paki, nig nog, chinky, blackie,
the fist comes down.
She's norra a paki blackie
she had her blood changed when she was born
Jenny sing-songs,
words tumble,
fist falls scramble
for a pigeon hole.

Hearing *Oi*, they leg it
down Lamb Street.
Jenny and me walk home.
She puts in my hand a red string
to her dog on wheels.
The shiny bobble tail on a spring wobbles
behind us.

Richard Scott
Maz

In the barbershop beneath my building
the boys are listening to Bengali rap.
A bearded one, perhaps nineteen, sharpens a cut-throat razor
upon an ancient leather belt
crisscrossed with cuts like a butcher's block
when a young man enters.

They shake hands, pull in for a half hug
then a towel is offered, tucked in around his athletics sweater.
The boy gestures to the smiling porcelain sink,
his thick forearm toned from the blade's repeated action,
then gently tilts his customer's head
against warm running water –
glittering like scales
caked on a fishmonger's palms.
He begins to lather. Suds run down the customer's muscular neck
and over the loops of his gang tattoo,
fingers slide in and out of wet soaped hair.

I can almost see my face
in the glistening black crew-cut.
I have stopped outside the shop window
in the otherwise empty street to watch.
The boy's eyes catch mine, he does not look away.
He knows why I am watching.

Rory Waterman
The Outings

I remember when this were covered in sheep
he said, his head full of meadow, his eyes on a car park/
supermarket/petrol station combo.
They hate it but it's cheap. Through the door-wheel they go.

Christmas is being made to last at the wrong end.
Past the frontline of pyramids of special biscuits
an obstruction of toys: they could kit themselves out
with pool table, ping-pong table, table-football table

but they're here for dad's big shop. And life now is split
into fortnights by afternoons like this.
And they're glad that nothing changes quite enough
to make them talk about it.

These hours are so familiar: the bleeping scanners;
the browsing at islands of cheese, at the reeking fish counter;
the quiet alleys of kitchenware; the reaching for tins;
the dozens and dozens of roasting chickens,

legs crossed on the spit, cartwheeling endlessly
in what seems like bliss; the cards and wrap
by the exit, all full of snow. And back through the doors
the feathery car-park trees, still more green than yellow.

Pascale Petit
Portrait of My Father as St Julien le Pauvre

You are reading *Le Monde* in the René Viviani Square.
You have thistles in your hair, earth blood on your clothes.
It is a sunny March morning, still early,
before they crowd in – the fountain of talking stags,
the pigeon you strangled as a boy, almost fainting with pleasure.
There's a bear near you with a knife in its heart,
a woodcock with its feet chopped off,
a bull with a hatchet through its ribs.
Polecats, lynxes, foxes, wolves –
you spear them all and more appear.

You spear them all and more appear –
polecats, lynxes, foxes, wolves,
a bull with a hatchet through its ribs,
a woodcock with its feet chopped off,
there's a bear near you with a knife in its heart,
the pigeon you strangled as a boy, almost fainting with pleasure,
before they crowd in – the fountain of talking stags.
It is a sunny March morning, still early.
You have thistles in your hair, earth blood on your clothes.
You are reading *Le Monde* in the René Viviani Square.

Amy Acre
The Ends of the Earth

for Amma

There has never been anything but this.
Winds blow seeds into bloom and in your mind
turn wheels and shapes I'll never understand.
Your sari tucked up to your waist. On the red fabric:
mud stains from forty years in the fields
with him, planting potatoes with sticks and string, your feet covered in
the scars of a life lived hard, raising heat-lazy babies.
You have earned your place at the head of this house with
the husband you were given to. Married at nine,
pregnant at fifteen: your belly stupa-solid – what else would you expect of
a woman who walked fourteen miles to the hospital in labour?
Gathering strength like the hems of skirts. You are a continent.
You speak a language all your own.
The sounds from your mouth bang drums through generations.
I can still hear you with one foot in the soil as
you kick sticks, and the world turns.

You kick sticks, and the world turns.
I can still hear you with one foot in the soil as
the sounds from your mouth bang drums through generations.
You speak a language all your own,
gathering strength like the hems of skirts, you are a continent,
a woman who walked fourteen miles to the hospital in labour.
Pregnant at fifteen (your belly stupa-solid) – what else would you expect of
the husband you were given to? Married at nine,
you have earned your place at the head of this house with
the scars of a life lived hard, raising heat-lazy babies
with him, planting potatoes with sticks and string, your feet covered in
mud stains from forty years in the field,
your sari tucked up to your waist. On the red fabric
turn wheels and shapes I'll never undenstand.
Winds blow seeds into bloom and in your mind
there has never been anything but this.

Miles Burrows
What to do After the Funeral

I dreamt the bus was going to Arcadia
And I was Death and I had missed the bus.

Uncle was to be cremated
At Gretna Green. It was to be
An elopement in flames with the Italian widow
He used to have lunch with in the underground restaurant
Opposite the Army and Navy Stores
Where they put too much water in the Campari
And he greeted the waiters in Italian
But they did not recognise him.
Finally among three synagogues
A cloister appeared looking out on a golf course,
And carved with the names of famous chefs.
Uncle as an old India hand
Would surely have been pleased
To share an incinerator with the Maharajah of Cooch Bihar.
Later, we walk to Novellino's down a side road,
Lamenting the loss of the King James version.
"They never use it these days, it's hopeless.
Bert's looking after someone's yacht in Greece. Aubrey
Is in pirate insurance so has had to dash."
Outside the restaurant on the pavement
Grappa out of polystyrene mugs
Avoids corkage. It's mushroom bruschetta.
Lucinda orders a *macchiato*. We copy her
As she seems to know what she's doing.

Julian Stannard
Lunch with Margot and Tinker

My stepfather the Duke of Bonheur
was twenty-nine
steps removed from
the Marquis de Sade
so I was beaten an awful lot
    said Tinker.

Anyway, said Margot
in that impeccable English
my father flew Junkers in the war
and he always had a plane
with enough fuel
to fly Hitler to Brazil.

    Tinker said:
Are you old enough
to remember
Sputniks over London?

Oh what a pity,
it was marvellous and
at the end of the street
there was a bunker.

    Margot said:
Can you imagine climbing
out of the bunker and looking
left and then looking right
and seeing nothing?

August Kleinzahler
Late Indian Summer

The rains hold off another week,
and the midday heat,
long after the winegrapes are in, has the cat
sprawled flat under the jade plant.

Nights already belong to winter.
You know by that tuning fork in its jacket
of bone
broadcasting to the body's far ports.

Days like this so late in the year
inflame desire, perturb
the ground of dreams, and roust us from sleep
exhausted and stunned.

Self-Criticism at 3 a.m.

Don't take that call:
Deft veronicas in an empty stadium,
The wind's applause ardent but fitful.

Ben Wilkinson
October

after Paul Verlaine

Here it comes now – autumn's cool evening –
the setting sun sparking leaves into life.
Death fills the fields with its single word
like the sudden *thwack* of a kitchen knife.

Wouldn't you wager it the truest season,
free of summer's delusional passions?
Watch it wait with its store of darkness
making sketches of all that might happen.

Of course those nutters and the pushovers
all go for spring and dawn, lovers who
looked a lot better the drunken night before.

Me? I'll take autumn's darkening glare
over any doe-eyed, angelic dove.
Its cold, sharp glance is the *real* look of love.

Joie de Vivre

after Paul Verlaine

Now you suckers and saps might fall for nature
but that confidence trickster doesn't fool me.
All those touched-up pastorals of half-assed
emotion are the last thing I want to see.

Art's a fucking joke, and we're no better –
I laugh at verse, the churches' fawning spires,
and worse, Canary Wharf's effervescence,
that Midas touch turning the whole lot to shit.

Assholes and good guys are one of a kind.
I've left behind faith, daydreams, and as for
love – *please*. Let's wave all that goodbye.

Like a useless toy boat that's miles offshore –
too tired to go on, but who can't pack it in –
I'll wait on the shipwreck still gunning for me.

Penelope Shuttle
Hvallator

You could live here forever
on Hvallator
without easy chair or clock,
plainsong of the four winds,

why not live here forever
on Hvallator, especially at low tide
when the beach is collected by hand,

wolf evenings
when you sing as you sew
down-lined comforters for the clergy,

you can live here forever, can't you,
it will keep the father quiet for hours,
tales of Imperial Russia at his beck and call,

wolves and foxes at home on Hvallator,
little green island, pressed flower of an island,
ten thousand dawns you will see, on Hvallator,
the voes at midnight shining like silver gauntlets.

Reading with Your Feet

IAN DUHIG

By way of Rebecca Solnit, I got to Lucy Lippard's note in *Overlay*, her study of relationships between contemporary and prehistoric art: "An Eskimo [*sic*] custom offers an angry person release by walking the emotion out of his or her system in a straight line across the landscape; the point at which the anger is conquered is marked with a stick, bearing witness to the strength or length of the rage." I do something similar except with bus; once, after reading yet another polarised "Here Be Dragons" projection map of contemporary poetry, I headed due north, eventually finding myself at the magnificent-sounding City of Troy, a small, unwalled turf maze in an area more famously landmarked by Shandy Hall or the Kilburn White Horse. I have been drawn back to it many times since. Its design seems to contain glimpses of antiquity, reminding me of roentgenizdats and Jorn's interest in mazy topological features, pursued in his book series *10,000 Years of Nordic Folk Art*. I don't believe the claims of great age for this particular Troy; although it is an argument from silence, I can't imagine Sterne not mentioning it if it existed in his lifetime, even in a digression – especially in a digression. However, I was deeply impressed by a local story that the maze's purpose is to lose the Devil, should he be pursuing you, because he can only move in straight lines, like a permanently angry man.

This morality story contradicts the well-known international narratives of salvation, which stress sticking to straight and narrow roads, avoiding distraction into backwaters and back alleys. Roads are languages, as they say, and poetry has many guides now, some of whom oversimplify the terrain in service of connecting up the landmarks, a natural human tendency: Stevens wrote of how we live in descriptions of places rather than the places themselves, while Lawrence observed, "the map appears more real to us than the land". Poetry's situation is certainly complex: the frayed threads of our pasts melt into Cage's river delta, his image of the arts reprised by George Szirtes in the last issue of this magazine against the idea of old man mainstream rolling along beside some overflow canals. However, poetry also shows us unmapped surprising and wonderful new worlds. I was wonderfully surprised to discover that the man who made the road the bus takes back to Leeds was blind from six – Jack Metcalf, who plundered Roman walls for stone and knew how to take poetic licence with the maps and plans of highway commissioners. The road passes near Andy Goldsworthy's old home, one of his "raw interfaces between city and country". Goldsworthy has spoken of "drawing a wall", a Klee taking a line for a walk but a line from Norman Nicholson (in 'The Wall That Went for a Walk') on journeys even more serendipitously random than Earnshaw's "surrealist expeditions" for which he might use this bus, where I once almost surrealistically heard children talking excitedly about poetry. There seemed to have been a series of events involving different kinds of poetry at their school and that day they were expecting Truth Maze, over from the USA. I had to google his name later to be sure I wasn't projecting some Shandean *nomen est omen* mishearing onto the schoolchildren's conversation. But no, I was able to appreciate their school's imagination in contacting him and enjoy online a sample of his astonishing vocal performances.

Brodsky wrote of the nomad's song as opposed to the prose of the farmer, and if music and poetry are not any more the sisters walking hand-in-hand that they were for Purcell, they are still close relatives in Leeds, where the biennial Lieder+ festival showcases collaborations between composers and poets. Leeds was also the late home of Darach Ó Catháin, whose astonishing vocal performances, prized so highly by Seán Ó Riada and Ciaran Carson, I enjoyed in The Roscoe on this same road. Mel Mercier, who brought Cage's *Roaratorio* to Huddersfield, enthused to Christopher Fox recently about Darach's singing, while Fox was researching his current project 'The Dark Road' about the motorway builders, one of whom was Darach. Leeds was the self-described "Motorway City of the Seventies", but always was a city of incomers, settling "like silt" in the local councillor's description.

For years now my interest has been repeatedly drawn back to a group of writers nurtured by the same community that hosted Truth Maze, Leeds Young Authors. You can't really generalise about their styles or subjects; trying to be helpful, one of them used the word "liminal" to describe their turf in an interview, but influences flow into LYA from all over the world. The Caribbean presence remains strong and watching LYA perform, I am often reminded of Derek Walcott's observation about the unfortunate loss of song in contemporary poetry. There are innumerable ways to sing but all song shares the sense of a line wrung and drawn out to multiply its implications in the labyrinth of the ear. I was therefore very interested to see how the LYA style would transfer to film in *We Are Poets*, which inevitably shows them vulnerable beyond their highly polished performances. When it was first shown locally some time ago, I watched it with my family sitting beside the poet Antony Dunn: we were all, well, amazed. The joint-directorial debuts of Alex Ramseyer-Bache and Daniel Lucchesi, it is an extraordinary, enriching

Leeds Young Authors: the team that flew to Washington, DC, in 2009. From the film *We Are Poets* (2012)

and encouraging picture, particularly relevant during the present governmental intervention in debates about poetry, education and the young. That *We Are Poets* was chosen to be shown at festivals around the world, winning Best Documentary awards at Ireland's 'Darklight' and the Sheffield film festivals, later came as no surprise. The 'Poets 4 Poets' fundraising initiative started there and then, which Antony worked so hard to establish and has now taken through its second successful year.

Talking to members of the audience after the first LYA fundraising reading was educational. It brought home to me the simple fact that places like Leeds just aren't big enough to sustain discrete and insulated coteries of poets outside the universities. Nevertheless, the achievements of LYA and *We Are Poets* have broken remaining ice and the meltwater from this is refreshing the delta, poets of every age and style. Jorie Graham in her recent *Spectator* interview (which also contains interesting reflections on our relationships with modern representations of reality) declared that poetry should be reclaimed by the oral tradition; in similar vein, one participant in *We Are Poets* suggested that a line could be drawn from their spoken poetry back to Homer. I had a flash of the White Horse of Kilburn beside its local turf Troy, as in Kavanagh's 'Epic', but it's not any kind of high horse (or a hobbyhorse) I want to get on here to offer yet another overview, magisterially pigeonholing the chaotic energies of this generation's poets, nor an underview in the manner of that "low theory" Wark describes as leading critique outwards "towards the labyrinth that is the production of situations". I don't really want to make any points at all – "the points are not the point, the poetry's the point", as you'll hear at LYA events. I want to to put in a word for pointless travelling without landmarks, like Jack Metcalf who could read with his feet, as Ovid was supposed to be able to do in the Sulmonese legend. It can be messy progress but poetry is messy and there are invaluable things to be found in the dark that you could not make up or discover in any other way – Ovid even danced in it, as many poets have done since. You have wonder and surprise to gain and nothing to lose but your certainties.

Ian Duhig has written six books of poetry, most recently *Pandorama* (Picador, 2010).

The Poet's Novel

PATRICK M^CGUINNESS

The phrase "A Poet's Novel" is often either pejorative (which is why anyone who uses it non-pejoratively quickly adds: "I don't mean in a bad way, of course...") or intended as the kind of compliment you could do without: that your book aspires to some higher realm where the basics of storytelling, plot and character development are mere impediments to some rarer purpose. We don't have a counterbalancing genre: there's no "novelist's poem", or at least the term doesn't exist. But the "Poet's Novel", while not being the most precise term in the lexicon, still tells us something about what to expect. Typically, the poet's novel will be overwritten, slack and meandering; it pauses for descriptive set-pieces that seem to stun the plot, substitutes mere consciousness in its *dramatis personae* for genuine, believable, character, and has problems with its length. By this I don't mean simply being too long or too short, but rather that it has difficulty inhabiting its length, the way an adolescent has difficulty inhabiting their body. For me, those flaws in the poet's novel are what make it interesting, what makes me seek it out: a discomfort with its form which isn't experimental (to be experimental you have to think you can master something) so much as strategically mutinous. The poet's novel never wants to dismantle and reinvent the novel, the way, say, Woolf or Proust or Joyce or Unamuno do. It just wants you to think it could if it wished to but on this occasion won't. Not all poets write poet's novels, and many poet's novels are written by people who aren't poets. As a sub-genre, it's not one that relies on its writer's occupation as such, but on the degree of ill-fittingness in the novel that makes the reader think its writer should probably have done something else, while still being glad the book exists. As a niche, there isn't a lot of room for manoeuvre.

My own novel owes its existence to its poetry hinterland, and would never have happened without it. Fiction and poetry didn't feel like separate genres, because of the constant bleeding of one into the other. I'd write a paragraph in prose, and then think about how it might work as a poem. I thought about a character, and imagined him or her writing a poem, which was often how I wrote poems anyway: imagining how someone who wrote poems might write about what was happening to me or inside me. For a time, this was good, but soon it got out of hand: there was so much bleeding across that, having started by trying to break down the borders between poetry and prose, I now needed to erect new ones, just to stop things from becoming unmanageable.

I started the novel with a set-piece description of arriving at Otopeni airport in Bucharest. I'd written a poem about that arrival in my first book, *The Canals of Mars*, 'Days in the New Country', in which the whole drama of the novel is compressed into a page and a half. The lines "Events hold their breath, as if unsure who / to happen to. Then they're overtaken by events" are basically my novel in a couplet. That, or the novel is the couplet expanded to four hundred pages. Either way, it's the same material.

Moving material across genres, from poetry into fiction and vice versa, felt like changing currencies at a border. Borders again: all my poems are about borders, and the novel was full of them too: a continuity of thematics I wasn't aware of while I was writing. The problem with changing currencies is that you have to reckon on all sorts of elements that eat into your original sum: the interest rate, the commission, the local taxes, the innate rapacity of the bureau de change, and so on. The novel suffered more than the poetry, because with prose it takes longer to see that something isn't working. But by the time you've worked out it isn't working, the material would be unusable on the other side of the border too. If I moved too much material back and forth, the material itself would dwindle: the process of exchange itself would destroy it.

You might be moving material across genres, but that material needed radically different treatment depending on which side of the border you were on. In fiction, you take longer run-ups. Your *bon mots* or your lapidary statements need to be *earned* (and that's how I thought of it: *earning* something, building the set), while your descriptions (so I thought) have to be instrumental, picking up the reader and depositing them further along the narrative arc. Characters have to be credible and whole, their motivations built up. In poetry it's different: your lines can be all tip and no iceberg, so long as they seem to imply a great mountain of thought and feeling below them, which they terminate, and for which they stand. In fact, ice cubes will do, provided you can arrange them to look like iceberg-tips. In narrative, I felt I had to write the icebergs too. How to get one character from one emotion to another? How to get one feeling to work itself through and finish where I wanted it to finish? My God, how was I even going to get people from one end of Bucharest to the other, let alone track their emotions and what they felt and thought as they did so? Someone's car pulls up and the door opens. How does it open? Which part of them will emerge first? The novel reader will want to know this, the poetry reader doesn't care. That's what I told myself, because I didn't know how to write novels.

Now I know that these are fake questions: the real novelist will make those moves, those jumps, those unexplained shifts, and no one will hold it against her because she does it well. It's not about providing the answers and explanations, it's about controlling the questions. I realised that too late. I should have thought more like a poet at precisely those moments when I was thinking myself into being a novelist, and besides, "thinking like a poet" and "thinking like a novelist" are false oppositions. "The reader will want to know..." I used to tell myself, because I thought that's how novelists thought. Really, if you do it right, the reader will want to know only what you want them to want to know. For this, it helps not to think about the reader at all.

There's another way in which borders were crossed: I invented a poet, Liviu Campanu, an apolitical exile stuck in Constanta and yearning with erotic melancholy for his mistress, a Party boss's wife back in Bucharest. Constanta is the modern name for Tomis, where Ovid spent his years of banishment, and in fact Campanu has what I described as an "Ovid Complex". People in the novel quoted him: "As Campanu said", they'd muse, or the narrator would think: "I recalled a line by the poet, Liviu Campanu", and so on. I wrote a few fragmented Campanu lines, iceberg-tips implying an oeuvre the size of an iceberg, and scattered them along the novel. He was seen only once, from afar, by the narrator, who remembered a couplet from one of his love poems and applied it to his own besottedness: "she was the trellis and I the vine / (which is a bourgeois poet's way of saying: I was all over her)". Campanu was a way, I thought, of insinuating poetry's "unearned" finishedness, its illusory wholeness, into the novel. The lines kept coming. Then, in one of my few acts of self-editing, I took Campanu out. As soon as he'd gone, I assembled his fragments on a page and set about writing whole poems around them. Before I knew it, I had about twelve pages of finished poems, which appeared in my second book, *Jilted City*, as pseudo-translations (I provided his biography and a scholarly edition) which I called 'City of Lost Walks' – the original title of my novel. Campanu is now a second self: I write poems as if I was him; I think through him, feel through him, and have written another twenty or so pages. It's I who have become his pseudonym. It's likely that my next book will be his: forged (in both senses of the word) in a novel, he continues to live in poetry. I think of his border-crossing as a kind of Cold-War defection between genres. I am now waiting for a Romanian translator to provide me with Campanu's originals.

Patrick McGuinness's poetry collections *The Canals of Mars* (2004) and *Jilted City* (2010) are published by Carcanet; his novel, *The Last Hundred Days* (Seren 2011), was longlisted for the Man Booker Prize, shortlisted for the Costa First Novel Award, and won the 2012 Wales Book of the Year Award.

To the Ends of the Earth

FIONA MOORE

Samantha Wynne-Rhydderch, *Banjo*, Picador, £9.99, ISBN 9780330544665
Nick Drake, *The Farewell Glacier*, Bloodaxe, £8.95, ISBN 9781852249335
Ian Pindar, *Constellations*, Carcanet, £9.95, ISBN 9781847770967
Mary O'Malley, *Valparaiso*, Carcanet, £9.95, ISBN 9781847771353

These books all have journeys as a theme and/or organising principle. Two poets went on real adventures – Mary O'Malley sailed on a marine research ship, and Nick Drake around Svalbard. Arctic explorers tell Drake's stories, and half of Samantha Wynne-Rhydderch's collection is narrated by Antarctic pioneers. Ian Pindar's journey is more a trajectory, from light to dark. Contemporary fears are explicit or implicit in all four collections: financial meltdown, climate change, the end of everything.

Samantha Wynne-Rhydderch writes very well about the strangeness of the world we have made for ourselves. In *Banjo* she has found an ideal subject. "We dug out / the quartz that had been Scott, Wilson // and Bowers, their lithologies in rock sequence", says Apsley Cherry-Garrard in 'Geology'. She has read *The Worst Journey in the World* and much else in order to write in the voices of six men from the Scott and Shackleton expeditions – a brilliantly imaginative re-telling of myth. She achieves this by focusing on the bizarre: objects and culture out of place (a piano, blacked-up theatricals); what happens in extreme situations. From 'Curtain Call':

> We've been taking it in turns
> to undo our shirts
>
> in minus seventy to nurse
> Oates's frostbitten foot
>
> on our breasts.

The six voices aren't distinct – rather a collective ghost-voice, classically British, humorous and reticent, that copes with adversity and speaks in rolling sentences or clipped phrases. Wynne-Rhydderch delights in specialist vocabularies and her use of ordinary words is unexpected. Occasionally this gets in the way of a poem. Mostly she carries it off. Floes around the

Endurance are "tenting up into starched hedgerows" in 'Greenheart'. In 'Cable-knit', a captain is "stitched up to the neck // in the intricacies of his sweetheart's cable-knit". Similar effects abound in the first half of *Banjo* (whose title works better after one has read the book), on general themes; there is also sadness here, in several moving elegies.

The Farewell Glacier is a book-length poem full of wonder and destruction, narrated by Arctic explorers from Pytheas the Greek onwards and by non-human speakers including methane and an ice-core sample. The wonder is expressed by Nick Drake's early explorers: "heather for our bedding / So we slept on the sweet scent of home / In the nowhere of the sea. / Our anchor was a stone / Dropped in bays of silence". Lack of enjambment and plain diction give the best passages a bardic tone reminiscent of the Anglo-Saxon poem 'The Seafarer'. There are some great stories. British explorer Wally Herbert walked across the sea ice from Alaska to Svalbard – "My Inuit friends left a map / Pinned to the hut door / Marked with the places they thought I would die."

Destruction is there from the first whalers: "Blood Sound. Stinking Sound". Non-humans take over at the end of the book, with mixed results, achieving most when they explain least. The haunting last piece, experimental in form, is an elegy for the Arctic, spoken by the shipping forecast in 2049. List-blocks are broken up with forecasts and a sea shanty, "Sing now and raise the dead / Time for us to go" (more can be heard at http://www.uva.co.uk/work/high-arctic#/10):

Greenland Sea	Sea of Okhotsk	Kara Sea
Baffin Bay	Arctic Basin	Canadian archipelago...
New ice	frazil ice	pancake ice
Brash ice	grey ice	white ice

Constellations ends with the end of the world: "Fade out. / Fade out to perpetual night, ending the era of light." That's poem 88; there are as many in Ian Pindar's book as constellations in the heavens. They move from light and summer through a love affair to instability, war, winter. All have two-, three- or four-line verses, with similar line lengths, assured, resonant line breaks and, in some poems, near-invisible end rhymes. The numbering and movement through six sections invite one to read from beginning to end; the metaphysical content and elegiac yet also authoritative tone might lead one to reflect on a poem each day – this is poetry to slow us down. Words and ideas reappear, differently, as if shaken in a starry kaleidoscope. The effect is often beautiful, though landscapes and ideas can seem generic or commonplace as they accumulate. Poem 30, which introduces chaos, brings a pleasurable shock:

> When the bottom fell out of the market, the oranges
> rolled down the hill, down the white lane.
> Each orange existed in its own light,
> complete in its geometry.

At their best, the poems in *Constellations* are striking and profound, driven by the energy of their thought and language. Poem 61: "What are poems but tests / in a landscape of thinking?"

Mary O'Malley's journey involves introspection and re-assessment in the middle of life, against the background of wider uncertainty and economic breakdown. Often she's without maps, driven by the need to leave, as in the second poem in *Valparaiso*, 'The Way', which characteristically blends lyricism with terse irony.

> No plans, just a cheap

> flight to some mythic city called Hotel
> or Airport. There are no countries left
> only the deep territories, the blackened hills.

"Impossible Ireland", country of so many earlier departures, is not spared. O'Malley is very good on the exasperation of living now, "the merchant class handing one another rosettes, / flanks heaving at how well we are doing / under the lash". That's from 'Sea Road, No Map', the first of several poems about her voyage on a research ship, where she finds "the kind of beauty / that leaves death unthinkable, / purple slate, gannets rising in small explosions".

Some of O'Malley's most memorable poems are short and highly concentrated – 'Tesseract' and the sonnet 'Caravaggio's Hands' on loss and love; 'Dreampoem II' on the housing bubble. Longer poems are most effective when they contain an eclectic mix of vivid imagery, and address modern life with wit and sarcasm. The ship goes nowhere near Valparaiso (I think it gets diverted, fittingly, to examine a toxic algal bloom). But it's departure and travel that matter. "Steer on by the Uncertainties."

Fiona Moore blogs at displacement-poetry.blogspot.co.uk; her pamphlet is forthcoming from Happen*Stance*.

The Weather in the Streets

TODD SWIFT

Dennis O'Driscoll, *Dear Life*, Anvil, £9.95, ISBN 9780856464461
Harry Clifton, *The Winter Sleep of Captain Lemass*, Bloodaxe,
£9.95, ISBN 9781852249359
Evan Jones, *Paralogues*, Carcanet, £9.95, ISBN 9781847771377
Peter Robinson, *The Returning Sky*, Shearsman, £8.95, ISBN 9781848611863

It would be hard to ignore the curiously thick cross-currents of themes, concerns and images that run through these four volumes, two from Irish poets and one apiece from an English and Canadian one. Most strongly there is the Banking Crisis, with its outriders Austerity and Bad Governance; but other shared affinities loom large, including echoes of Eliot and Yeats, exiles in return, poets in unexpected places (Cavafy in Liverpool, Rimbaud in Reading, Robinson in LA), and lots of weather. There is also love; there usually is.

Dennis O'Driscoll is a poet who strikes me as beginning to resemble a Celtic Billy Collins, for good and ill. His *Dear Life* is a thoroughly engaging, often bleakly funny collection that exhausted me at its full length: as with many a charming dinner guest, fewer self-aware bon mots might have actually been more. The problem is, I think, that O'Driscoll now knows he has an audience, and knows what his sort of poem is and can do – and then goes ahead and does it. Though his way with metaphor is nothing short of clever – butterflies are "package tourists bounding / through Arrivals in Hawaiian shirts", swallows are "tax exiles" – sometimes this will to wit is tedious, obvious: winter has a "scorched-earth policy" and sleeping men have penises at "half mast, a complete flop". Generalisations abound: "God gets nothing right these days" in 'Last Stand' and, in one of several sometimes easy list poems, 'Synopsis', "Life passes at a breakneck rate". One wants to say, tell me something new. O'Driscoll also has a habit – and I realise this is an aspect of his work that has been praised in the past – of finding a quasi-metaphysical way of comparing everything in nature and existence to office-related matters. The inflated jargon of the business world is well punctured here, but sometimes it seems a stretch: life is a "ruthless boss", spring is a "short-term vision". Then again, when his poems stop trying to find their satirical correlatives in the fallen world of Mammon, they are often moving, however much they are still about the workaday world, as in the pitch-perfect 'Time

Enough': "The tally of years / added up so rapidly / it appeared I had / been short-changed, / tricked by sleight / of hand, fallen victim / to false bookkeeping." This, his ninth collection, confirms O'Driscoll as a comic master of the kind of poem that, recently, Kevin Higgins has also been perfecting – the sub-prime Larkin.

Harry Clifton's new collection was an eye-opener for me, revealing the extent to which the poems he is currently writing set him up as one of the major Irish poets of our time. There is no other way to read this marvellously deep, rich and powerful book, so tangled with history, lyricism and shaping intelligence, than in assent. Convincing in its moods, its tempos, its weathers, *The Winter Sleep of Captain Lemass* traverses in time the struggles of Ireland since, roughly, the Easter Rising, and in space mainly – as its sections indicate – "twenty-six counties", "six counties" and "elsewhere". As in his previous, award-winning *Secular Eden*, this is a book that takes the measure of things – and the Irish present is found sorely lacking.

The overall statement seems to be, Ireland has been robbed blind many times before, and has suffered, but look what it has, even still, even now. In 'The Year of the Yellow Meal' starvation is described as "Our theology". We are shown "all those towns named Dysart", meaning desert. There is "radio silence" and "mizzling rain". These are the end of some days, for sure, but despite the flood imagery of the book's last lines – "Crashed out, under travelling Irish skies, / Wondering is it here the waters rise" – there is hope in the resurrection rhyme of skies/rise. Indeed, like the best of Beckett, whose bleak comic lyricism Clifton shares, this collection's emphasis on stark conditions never impoverishes, but rather, in its lean gaze, recovers what remains after much, even most, is taken or simply gone. There are several great poems here, consciously summoning Yeats in his more austere mode, including the superb 'Dying Generations' with its echo of a crazy salad and meat. Here are its closing lines: "... I no longer believe in anything / But the greenness, the greyness, / The eternal everydayness / Of Ireland. Time, they tell me, will come back – / The past, the future. Meanwhile I wake / With an empty mind, to a high ceiling, / A jug of clear spring water, / The buzz of a chainsaw, somebody felling a tree."

Clifton's book arises in part from the return-of-the-native syndrome (he'd been away for sixteen years), as does Peter Robinson's *The Returning Sky* (a Poetry Book Society Recommendation). Robinson had been in Japan, and then came back to England and its "eternal everydayness". Though the work can sometimes seem bleached out or humdrum, like Larkin without the humour or the epiphanies, I don't think any other English poet currently writing is leaving as true, if depressed, a picture of what it looks like to be alive now in England. I mean this literally, reductively – his work is compulsively driven to record, often in minute detail, the English weather, so that you really see the rain, the dull skies, and feel the heavy fug of the times. The book feels slightly overlong, but a handful of the poems are as good as anything he, or anyone else now writing, have done, and these tend to pinpoint their emotional intensities, so we know why the Robinson weather matters. Here is the fourth stanza of the title poem: "Now our lately dead are in the air. / An overcast grey-scale dusk's / shot through with thin red cloud streaks; / and, look, they're everywhere / in privet hedges, like a private grief / for the targeted to die." In this poem, and others like '120 Addington Road' and 'Mortgaged Time', Robinson shows why he is a major English poet, whose enigmatically insubstantial land- and cloudscapes reveal more than they veil.

Evan Jones is a bit of an exiled poet himself, or one returning home, or both, and plays with this sort of identity in his first British collection – he is better known in Canada, where his first book was a finalist for the equivalent of the UK's T.S. Eliot Prize. Though his name sounds Welsh, he is Canadian by way of Greece (he is a dual citizen) and has lived in Britain since 2005, and cosmopolitanism is one of the main themes of this smart and allusive book. Perhaps the wittiest of the poems is the brief sequence 'Mr Eugenides, The Smyrna Merchant', which rather rescues that character from Mr Eliot. The most ambitious is the sequence of 24 meta-fictive poems, 'Constantine and Arete: An autobiography', which shows that Jones is fully aware of the modernist mythic method, interpenetrating the past and the present, poignantly. If Jones is to be faulted, it is perhaps in the dandyish assuredness of his felicities – he seems almost primly pleased with his ability to point up the painted backdrops of some of his poems, as in 'Little Notes On Painting'. But his finest poem here, 'Cavafy in Liverpool', manages to escape its potential post-modern burdens and sing:

> Here is your sad young man:
> he is ship-to-shore, he is buttoned-down
> in tweed and scarved, eyes closed
> when the Mersey wind
>
> calls his collar to his ear
> on the strand near Albert Dock,
> some January, some winter day
> we recognize but take no part in.

Todd Swift's eighth and latest poetry book is *When All My Disappointments Came At Once* (Tightrope Books, Toronto, 2012).

Unlit Rooms

MICHAEL HULSE

Lesley Saunders, *Cloud Camera*, Two Rivers Press, £8.99, ISBN 9781901677812
Stephen Edgar, *The Red Sea. New & Selected Poems*, Baskerville,
$19.95, ISBN 9781880909782

Anyone who reads contemporary poetry needs these important books. The poets could hardly be more different. Lesley Saunders is arresting for the vigour with which her thought compels words. Stephen Edgar is striking for his cadenced grace. Each is dazzling, and each should be far better known.

The poet of *Cloud Camera* knows about "the portable ache of self", and knows that the world of dreams and desires co-exists with the world of empirical data. She can generate excitement out of that understanding. That is what makes Lesley Saunders extraordinary. Anyone can write about dreams, and anyone can write about data. But not everyone, contemplating an anatomical model, can move from "Apparently I am made of parts. A locked box of troubles" to this conclusion: "I am unlit rooms, a visionary anatomy shaken by small fevers. / How I live is dark science, fretful fugue; a mirror under a shawl." The rigour that goes into "I am unlit rooms" is worthy of a Donne.

Science means knowing, and poetry about knowing – philosophical poetry – is one of the oldest traditions in writing. To write about the man who holds the record for the longest and fastest sky-dive, or Fanny Burney's mastectomy, is like writing about the shield of Achilles, in Lesley Saunders's hands: that is, it becomes a profound inquiry into the nature of experience and knowledge. The dynamism of her responses, across a wide emotional and factual spectrum, makes *Cloud Camera* the most intelligent and thrilling book of poetry I've seen in several years.

Don't take my word for it. See her poem on Mary Shelley's dream that her dead baby came to life, her poem on the fallen angels (whose knowledge is "not to be unlearned now"), or these last lines of 'Census':

> If this is not the life you meant to live, please ask
>
> for help. We belong to the beloved. How would you
> describe. How well can you speak. How long can you stay.

Lesley Saunders is distinguished in her first field, educational research. *Cloud Camera* should place her among those who are seriously spoken of in her second calling, poetry. Was it not submitted to the PBS, that this book failed to be a Choice?

Australia's Stephen Edgar appears here in a pared-back US selection from several earlier books, with fifteen new poems, and on the jacket there's Clive James's praise of his eloquence and beauty and August Kleinzahler's of his elegance and depth. Edgar is as adept as Saunders at imprinting a personal passion onto objective material. Where she probes and excavates, he enacts and performs. His arguments-with-himself are an unfolding, a revealing, a thinking-aloud. In 'Vertigo', four stanzas deliberate on the obliteration of past time, only to reach this wonderful fifth:

> What if, as Russell joked, the world was made
> Just now, with stores
> Of memory placed within us to persuade
> Belief in preterite fullness and past age –
> Like that old notion that the Earth is young
> But came with fossils of the dinosaurs
> Compressed and slipped among
> The pictures on its fresh, God-doctored page.

Yes, Edgar recalls Wilbur and Hecht, and sometimes Stevens, and poems dedicated to countrymen Les Murray and Robert Gray underscore the serious, and seriously Australian, nature of his tussle with the place of art, and the place of the human, in the global system. This isn't poetry for those who crave the open microphone. It's the real thing – ambitious yet modest, wry but whole-hearted, graceful, genuine, open.

Michael Hulse's latest book is the anthology, *The Twentieth Century in Poetry* (Ebury, 2011), co-edited with Simon Rae.

Late Light on Reality Street

PETER HUGHES

Ken Edwards, *Bardo*, Knives Forks and Spoons Press, £8, ISBN 9781907812729
Carol Watts, *Occasionals*, Reality Street, £8.50, ISBN 9781874400523
Maggie O'Sullivan, *Waterfalls*, Reality Street, £9, ISBN 9781874400578
Anne Carson, *Antigonick*, Bloodaxe, £15, ISBN 9781852249397

The Knives Forks and Spoons Press is an energetic and adventurous outfit. Ken Edwards's *Bardo* is a striking example of their output. It's a rewrite of the *Tibetan Book of the Dead*, suitably updated, and now set in Hastings. The original was a devotional text to help the dead resist reincarnation. Edwards's version is full of ghosts, edges, instability. It is also crammed with wit, contemporary detail and vertiginous shifts in scale: "Light had travelled for 10 to 15 billion years from the early universe. There was then mayhem for about five minutes, after which most of the cut flowers, pies and cakes had gone." Part of the material for the book seems to come from Edwards moving house, and this is made to chime with the spirits of the recently dead hovering between worlds. The text is full of change. Light from over the sea, the shifting colours and patterns of the sea itself, light bending through rooms and memories: all is transient. At a key point one character observes, "It's about making sense of it, making a story before it's too late. But... it's always too late." *Bardo* manages to be luminous, funny and philosophical all at the same time.

Ken Edwards's own press, Reality Street – which was formed from two other presses founded by Edwards and Wendy Mulford in the 1970s – will celebrate its 20th anniversary next year. It has published key works by Tony Baker, Kelvin Corcoran, Allen Fisher, Fanny Howe, Tony Lopez, Denise Riley, Peter Riley, Lisa Robertson and Maurice Scully, alongside work by Ken Edwards himself and many other independent spirits. The press has also published several distinctive works of prose, including books by John Hall, Paul Griffiths, David Miller, John de Wit and Doug Oliver. The latter's *Whisper 'Louise'* is ambitious, moving and experimental: an exemplification of the Reality Street project. Another important aspect of the press has been its two anthologies. The influential *out of everywhere*, edited by Maggie O'Sullivan, samples the work of thirty women poets working adventurously with language. The second eye-opening anthology was *The Reality Street Book of Sonnets*, edited by Jeff Hilson. *The Alchemist's Mind*, an anthology of poets writing narrative prose, edited by David Miller, is due out in November.

Carol Watts's *Occasionals* is a kind of Shepherd's Calendar, registering four seasons. Sixty-eight poems of twenty eight lines each are grouped as: *autumncuts, wintercuts, springcuts* and *summercuts*. Each poem is dated to a specific day. The linguistic environment of the day is sampled, collaged, reflected upon. Thoughts are interrupted by overheard phrases and new thoughts. Natural processes, anticipations, flits of panic, unexpected full stops: the poems surf the bitty experience of thinking, and thinking about thinking, and wondering how much of this can be gathered, harnessed, or simply enjoyed, attended to. I was reminded of Charles Olson's famous dictum: "One perception must immediately and directly lead to a further perception." As in *Bardo*, new data and reflections keep flooding in and the writing moves on, attending where it can, but developing its own musics and momentum: "Leaving notes to himself, a mark of later / incorporation, and you. Need not be too bashful, / speak your mind, or name. Something gives you the / right to speak, what. Can feel like a blaze, half-lit. / Moon brighter, the smoke of the sky. halo. He said..."

Maggie O'Sullivan's *Waterfalls* comes from the very edge of speech, sound and song in ways which seem both modern and archaic. We are made unusually aware of the physicality of words, both in terms of their disposition on the page (the typography is far from conventional), and in terms of their mouthed sounds, the physical means of production. If you get the chance to hear O'Sullivan read you should take it – and these days it just takes a couple of clicks to find her recordings on the internet. There is a startling sense of language being drawn from near its origins, fetched from far margins. The extremes are not merely linguistic. There are suggestions of chant, of dislocated ritual, of voices reaching the limits of conscious thought. There are voices dying too, especially in passages gesturing back to the famine in Ireland: "low ground long black crepe rolled in the mouth's threshing / gleam and misty blood dripping so many red threads / the maps are become / ... round round as an O's hoop scouring vowels – ..." Maggie O'Sullivan's parents were from the west of Ireland and this book is dedicated to the memory of her father. We are a long way from the trim, conventional comforts of much mainstream poetry here. The pages echo ancient cries and bring together wild and unkempt musics.

All the work reviewed here has learned from various versions of Modernism how to incorporate the complexities of contemporary experience. This holds true of Anne Carson's new translation of Antigone too. Consider the very first lines: "[Enter Antigone and Ismene] Antigone: We begin in the dark and birth is the death of us   Ismene: Who said that

Antigone: Hegel   Ismene: Sounds more like Beckett".

You may sometimes be startled to see your own fingers moving behind the translucent pages which punctuate this handsome, eerie book. The text is presented as Carson's own handwriting, in capitals. The illustrations veer off from the text at tangents, and include modern electrical appliances. Much of the text is raw, like bleeding chunks of language. Carson lost a brother in painful circumstances (her earlier work *Nox* is a bold and unconventional tribute to him), and her empathy with the plight of Antigone is palpable. The savagery of Sophocles' drama spits off the page: "seven spears in his mouth instead of teeth". The impact is exceptional, long-lasting, genuinely dramatic. Perhaps we should end with the final advice of the Chorus: "Last word wisdom better get some even too late."

Peter Hughes's *Selected Poems* will be published by Shearsman in 2013, together with a volume of responses to his work, edited by Ian Brinton.

ℬ

A View from the Train

TIM DOOLEY

Incorrigibly Plural: Louis MacNeice and his Legacy, ed. Fran Brearton and Edna Longley, Carcanet, £18.95, ISBN 9781847771131

Developing steadily since his early death in 1963, Louis MacNeice's reputation as a poet has grown exponentially in the last decade and a half. His early shorter poems, particularly 'Snow', have become such touchstones for a particular magic lyricism that quotation from them is in danger of sliding from familiarity to cliché. This collection of essays by contemporary poets and scholars mixes celebration and re-evaluation judiciously, capturing the tone of MacNeice's current relationship with his successors while opening up lines of discussion which may make MacNeice's work interesting in different ways over the decades to come.

A major feature of his recent ascendancy has been a stronger emphasis on MacNeice's Northern Irish roots; in Brearton and Longley's words, his "first world underlies the rest". Certainly Northern Irish poets – particularly Michael Longley, whose excellent selection of MacNeice's poetry is available in Faber's *Poet to Poet* series, and Derek Mahon, whose early poem 'In Carrowdore Churchyard' celebrated a "play of shadow", "humane perspective" and "fragile, solving ambiguity" in MacNeice's legacy – have, in choosing MacNeice as a significant antecedent for their project, played an important part in securing the continuity of his relevance.

Paul Muldoon's *Faber Book of Contemporary Irish Poetry* (1986) hinted, however, at a riddling rather than solving ambiguity in the act of claiming the poet for a mainly Irish tradition, printing as its prologue a transcription of a radio discussion from 1939 in which MacNeice responds to F.R. Higgins:

> I have the feeling that you have sidetracked me into an Ireland versus England match… no doubt this was very good for me. However, I am still unconverted.

'Valediction', 'Neutrality' and sections of 'Autumn Journal' reveal the difficulty MacNeice had in identifying himself with the Ireland of his time, either North or South. Paul Farley, in his contribution to this collection, quotes from MacNeice's incomplete autobiography *The Strings Are False*:

> My parents came from (the) West or, more precisely, from Connemara, and it was obvious that both of them vastly preferred it to Ulster… So for many years I lived on a nostalgia for somewhere I had never been.

Farley identifies with this sense of 'being twice removed from his familial source', linking it to a characteristically modern anxiety about identity. Nick Laird notes that MacNeice "lived everywhere as a foreigner" and recalls how MacNeice's "disenfranchisement" enabled the younger poet to challenge "received narratives" as a teenager in mid-Ulster during the 1980s and 1990s.

Hugh Haughton, Terence Brown, Stephen Regan and Leontia Flynn focus in different ways on movement and travel in MacNeice's work. Haughton, in perhaps the most convincing of the academic essays here, sees MacNeice as "one of the first poets… to see the world through the eyes of a driver, a passenger and an observer of traffic, as attentive to roads and railways as the landscape they take him through", and draws on the sociologist John Urry's theory of mobilities to link that interest to an unsettling modernist concern with instability and flux. Haughton is one of a number of contributors to *Incorrigibly Plural* who draw attention to 'Star-gazer', a poem from MacNeice's final collection in which the speaker remembers, forty-two years earlier, running from one side to the other of a non-corridor train looking at constellations and trying out their Latin names. The best part of a lifetime later, he observes that the light from the stars:

> will never arrive
> In time for me to catch it, which light when
> It does get here may find that there is not
> Anyone left alive
> To run from side to side in a late night train
> Admiring it and adding noughts in vain.

(Paul Farley gives an account of trying to replicate this experience but finding it impossible in "current South West trains rolling stock".)

Incorrigibly Plural contains several attempts to explore analogies between MacNeice's work and that of other poets. Farley plumps surprisingly for John Clare; Stephen Regan makes a solid case for MacNeice's influence on Larkin, while Paul Muldoon finds affinities with Frost and Yeats. There is interesting focus on technique in Neil Corcoran's essay on repetition and Glyn Maxwell's illuminating study of the form of 'Autumn Journal'. Clair Wills and John Goodby each make a stab at opening up discussion of MacNeice's largely ignored "middle stretch" between the mid-1940s and the 1950s. Wills examines 'Autumn Sequel' in the context of MacNeice's work for the BBC, while Goodby explores MacNeice's friendship with Dylan Thomas in terms of literary kinship – arguing that the two poets shared "an older more inclusive poetic culture" than has existed since. Goodby asserts that later conditions created "a situation... in which it became possible for so-called 'mainstream' and 'alternative' poetries to ignore each other". It's not the most convincing of arguments, but its attempt to reclaim MacNeice's work for modernism has at least the virtue of originality.

Brearton and Longley include several pieces of historical or biographical interest. Anne Margaret Daniel uses T.S. Eliot's correspondence among other sources to give us insight into the marketing of MacNeice in the United States during the 1940s, while David Fitzpatrick attempts to clarify the one-nation Unionism of Frederick MacNeice, Louis's father, the Bishop who stood out against a Union Jack being used at the funeral of the partitionist Carson. Perhaps the pieces that give greatest pause for thought in *Incorrigibly Plural*, however, are the two brief memoirs by the son of the poet written initially for private purposes, but completed for publication shortly before his death in 2009. At nineteen Dan MacNeice had chosen to live with his mother in the United States, rather than stay with the father who had brought him up haphazardly enough since she had abandoned the home a year after Dan's birth. His account of his final parting with Louis echoes the themes of uncertain identity, travel and solitariness which run through MacNeice's work and this often engrossing book:

I think we both realised at this moment of parting that in some ways we had never really known each other and that each had failed the other in our relationship, probably from the fear of closeness. Then he gave me a scarf which I put away carefully like a religious relic and wore for the first time when I visited his grave almost thirty years later. The train pulled away and we never met again.

Tim Dooley's poems are collected in *Keeping Time* and *Imagined Rooms*, both published by Salt. He is reviews editor for *Poetry London*.

&

Lose Yourself in Strange Lands

ANDRÉ NAFFIS-SAHELY

Ruth Padel, *The Mara Crossing*, Chatto & Windus, £12.99, ISBN 9780701185558

Poets may not drive, but they certainly travel, and before even opening this book I knew Padel had her adventurer's credentials down pat. In *Tigers in Red Weather* (2005), the record of her two-year quest across Asia on the lookout for tigers, Padel went kayaking down the Mekong and rode an elephant in the Bengali Sundarbans. Ostensibly a work of non-fiction – the usual genre demarcations becoming increasingly irrelevant in her work – Padel presented the reader with a satisfying blend of travel writing, memoir and natural history, proving herself an exemplary researcher. Continuing in this tradition, *The Mara Crossing*, Padel's ninth collection, is a virtuoso summation of her varied interests: from genetics to Greek myths and birdwatching, interests which Padel binds together with zoological detail around her chosen theme: migration.

From the "prologue", where Padel explains her choice of the *prosimetrum* – "a literary genre which combined prose and poetry" – as her medium, to reflections on her own family origins, *The Mara Crossing* is as epic a journey as they come; from "a parked jeep on a riverbank in Kenya" to Scotland and the South Pacific, and everything in between, all the way to "the planet's largest migration" when "billions of jellyfish rise to the surface to feed and sink back down at dawn", *The Mara Crossing* is a compassionate study of how migration – both human and animal – "made the world".

Padel's decision to employ the *prosimetrum* deserves high praise: each prose section serves as a pit stop for Padel to introduce her topics before focusing in with her poetic lens. Fortunately, though she certainly gets her facts straight, Padel's poetry never gets buried under the science and we get a firm sense of emotion running throughout. The opening lines of 'Nocturne' are a case in point:

> Sundown. I imagine my father,
> ten years dead, examining the lilied deep,
> a whole marine community
> on the move while the planet sleeps.

The light Padel sheds on the course of her own migration opens a Kafkaesque window into our disordered world, at times turning into a catalogue of countless scarred or truncated lives:

> You're on Dead Island: a Detention Centre.
> The Russian refugees who leaped from the fifteenth floor
> of a Glasgow tower block to the Red Road
> Springburn – Serge, Tatiana and their son
> who when immigrations officers
> were at the door, tied themselves together
> before they jumped – knew what was coming.

'Children of Storm', the penultimate prose section, features some of the book's most startling visuals. After describing the grim realities of the 'Border Fence Project', perhaps the greatest living proof of American xenophobia, which purportedly aims to stem the tide of illegal immigration from Mexico into the United States, Padel takes us on a bizarre tangent involving video games:

> [...] there is now an iPhone game about driving illegal migrants
> into the United States. In *Smuggle Truck* you dodge bullets from
> the drug mafia and border guards, tilt your pickup to catch babies
> bouncing out at the back as your cargo gives birth, and get them
> to the border where 'The Star-Spangled Banner' strikes up and
> you get your green card – and your score.

Details such as this make *The Mara Crossing* one of the most eccentric and eclectic books in recent memory. There are few poets writing today with such a sophisticated grasp of language and such a brazen willingness to engage with the big, important issues, merging the light, gentle touch of nature writing with brutal observations about the human condition.

The Mara Crossing likely benefited from Padel's work on Darwin: A Life in Poems (2009), written in tribute of her ancestor's bicentenary, which has in turn given The Mara Crossing a stylistic and thematic wholeness that was somewhat absent in her earlier collections. "Seek oneself, lose oneself in strange lands! But with a guiding line, with bread crumbs or white pebbles!" says Joaquim Font in Bolaño's The Savage Detectives – and reading The Mara Crossing is like picking up those crumbs or pebbles as we wind our way through Padel's unsettling wood. This is her finest book yet.

André Naffis-Sahely is a poet and translates from the French and the Italian. His translation of Émile Zola's L'argent is forthcoming from Penguin Classics.

A Living Form

DAVID MORLEY

Pamphlets published by Happen*Stance* (www.happenstancepress.com), Oystercatcher (www.oystercatcherpress.com), Rack Press (http://rackpress.blogspot.co.uk), Donut (www.donutpress.co.uk), Knives Forks and Spoons (www.knivesforksandspoonspress.co.uk) and Smith/Doorstop (www.poetrybusiness.co.uk)

Spring 2012: I post nano-reviews on Facebook and Twitter. Aim: to capture emerging poets' oeuvres as essences, centres: torchlight thrown in one sentence. Crossword-clue prose. Dalek diction. Shrew-quick lit-crit. Result? Facebook Shares. Thumb-up Likes. Retweets. Retreats. Summer 2012: comes a book bundle, many and various pamphlets, limited word count. Possible? Plausible. If all elided and prose goes plate-spin. Seek a form. Write long; sculpt short. Not notes but distillations. As pamphlet plies essence, criticism must be shorn bone.

HAPPENSTANCE PRESS. Pamphlets beguiling objects. Eye-made. Joy to hold, read. Spinning Plates (2012): Richie McCaffery's tercets tightly judged yet talk to heart. Blurb ("words like rare marbles – see them roll!") unpicks admirable perception:

> Somewhere in God's granite allotment plots,
> nanotechnologies of hatred and grudges
> were stirring the blessed, restful soil.   'The Rapture'

Arson (2011): Sue Butler possesses great range and resource: "...rate the pain. *As Keaton is slapstick, / Akhmatova grief.* What eases it?" Butler is an Angel of Italics. Loved chemistry in 'Hard': equation as nano-poetry. Heaven's hell of title poem: "*I soak your lies / in petrol* (strum), / *post them lit / through your letter box* (strum)". *Close* (2012): Theresa Muñoz's "less is more" poetics define and defy space; deify the quotidian (*Greggs Bakers*, Waverley station, East Preston Street Cemetery); a Vasko Popa game-like eye for movement and line:

> now
> walking fast
> away
>
> hands in pockets
> fresh air
>
> *who cares   who cares   who cares*
>
> but I do   'Performance Review'

Blackbirds (2012): Christina Dunhill's a genuine find, although admired for years in magazines and *Anvil New Poets 1995*. A *Springwatch* of a mind; Wallace Stevens, Englished. Intricate, pin-sharp observed natural worlds: 'Blackbirds' ends:

> Along the stripes blackbirds come bobbing
>   hopping down and stopping short
>
>   hopping backwards back again
>   and bobbing out
>
> like thoughts we had and then thought better of
> and then thought better of the thinking better of.

After the Creel Fleet (2011): Niall Campbell's skilfully sprung pamphlet of terse, purposeful, sharp poems. Enviable precision. Don Paterson presides ("And here, Boccaccio, fool, I talk of love"), but Campbell's his own man. Full collection essential. *Taking Account* (2011): Peter Gilmour's complete surrender of self in heartbreaking territory is superbly measured. His wife's suicide and aftermath hugely affecting, brilliantly kindled as form and language.

OYSTERCATCHER PRESS. Michael Marks Award highly justified. Fascinating range of writers and scrupulously edited. *The Son* (2009): Carrie Etter's sparkling, serious beating-out of prose poetry and catechism continues in a finely judged sequence, grieving and honouring and surprising on every page. "It is time" (Etter quotes Celan) "the stone made an effort to flower". And so this fine book, its respect, sadness and subject. *Kiss Off* (2011): Sophie Mayer used Facebook as crafting tool with delectable dare. A performance for ear and eye, mind and body. Impishly realised. Finesse of sound and repetitive devices make poems sing, buzz, even ring:

> in a doublet and farthingale
> in a black tux and nylons
> in an island nightclub
> in a shower a singlet.   'Third Attempt] (ExtraIrigaray)'

The Reluctant Vegetarian (2009): Richard Moorhead. Rapt by four seasons realised through fruit and veg: sounds potty; *is* party to genius; smart inventiveness in terms of structure and stability of images, language and ideas. Takes organic subject and teases, tickles and tortures: cabbages, figs, parsnips, peaches, sugarsnaps et al, pulling metaphors from them like lines of protein-nanoparticle-rabbits-from-hats. Bio-layer interferometry is the new poetry. *The Lotion* (2010): Sophie Robinson's firework-box of a pamphlet ("My paper-veins, match-lit"): urgent, deliciously sensual and arresting. Cover image: punk poetry of itself. Merry Melodies madness afoot: "a stapler greeted / By skin, broke, fell to earth like a gazelle". A gazelle? Yikes. The same might be exclaimed of *Happy Whale Fat Smile* (2010): Ralph Hawkins for whom Blake's "energy is eternal delight" is fuel for serious play and verbal display in sequential single poem: "Pleasant things are always sensual" he writes after stating: "Soon young men will want wombs / And women cocks so they can piss at different angles." Quite. Manic fun and magical logic throughout. *Behoven* (2009): Peter Hughes simply, startlingly delights with "these registrations of the 32 Beethoven piano sonatas". How? Now! Poems sway, tinkle and crescendo. Don't be alarmed when eye is yanked by shape-shifting manoeuvres; go with Hughes's deft, superfine fingering. Trust him.

RACK PRESS ever impresses, picking up emerging and fledged poets and letting the taut form of a pamphlet test them into experiment, close-argued arrangement and sequence, as here in these limited editions. *The Heretic's Feast* (2012): Michèle Roberts's pamphlet hosts five poems in memory of her mother: a series of concise movements irrupting into epiphanies, the whole making a satisfying poem from the individual memories. An unconsoling yet illuminating concerto of reflective grief. *House of Blue* (2012): Denise Saul's work highly striking, intelligent and various. Exile and inner-exile. Title poem held me, would not let me go; ditto 'Leaving Abyssinia' – mesmeric final stanza. *Spring Journal* (2012): Dan Wyke's appealing diary-like poetry of observations and philosophising: miniature becomes miraculous; quotidian is sacralised. Wyke nails his poetic terms (and himself to a fence-top) in first sequence:

> What I don't say
> > is what I really mean.
> What I am unable to say
> > I mean most of all.

'Days of March', second sequence: exquisite maze of March days and self-regardingly funny: "There's only this life; / go and buy James Tate's Selected Poems / and stop waiting for the price to go down". Wyke understands that the pamphlet is itself a form of poetry. *Oh Bart* (2012): Martina Evans: under-rated poet or overlooked? – maybe makes her more free in subject and tone, as here in poems that range and dance over religion, education, *The Simpsons* and *The Godfather*. "Prayer, the last refuge of the scoundrel", she quotes Lisa Simpson: Evans's subject in fabulously elastic, strongly voiced lines. Bernard O'Donoghue right as ever: "total clarity with profundity", and let me add how hilarious Evans can be.

DONUT PRESS. Possibly the most tantalising of the newer independent presses for sky-high production values (two pamphlets here in plastic bags to preserve them against humanity) and a stable of wide-awake poets. *The Camden Art Redemption Miracle* (2011): droll fly-on-the-wall account of the process of roguish conceptual art; I will never watch *The Aristocats* with the same eyes. Tim Turnbull distinctive as one of the most inventive new poets; certainly one of the more artful. *Apocrypha* (2011): A.B. Jackson's sequence a convincing verbal sound-show with surprising imagery and deft rhythmical switch-backing: "Bed-head Lazarus, at breakfast: / three Embassy Regal, tea so strong / you could trot a mouse on it." Intelligent, wonderfully-heard act of writing: a concept album with sleeve notes on authorial process: "Thanks to the staff and management of The Pot Still on Hope Street, Glasgow, for keeping my various pads of A4 foolscap behind the bar". *Beloved, In Case You've Been Wondering* (2011): Wayne Holloway-Smith exacts poise, purpose and variety of a full collection from a pamphlet. How? By mega-mixing. By altering tone throughout. By deploying personae, fictional and real characters. By tall stories, epistles, dramatic monologues. A notable concentration of talent.

KNIVES FORKS AND SPOONS PRESS. Their mission: to show that the underground poetry scene is as important (whatever that may mean) as the mainstream (whatever that might be these days). Persistently productive; lacklustre production values compared to Donut, Rack, Happen*Stance* and Oystercatcher (or for that matter: Five Leaves, Lapwing, Longbarrow, Mariscat, Salt, Shoestring, tall-lighthouse, Templar and Two Rivers). USPs of Knives, Forks and Spoons? Playground energy, eclecticism and international avant-garde. At best they possess a brilliant sense of adventure; at worst, they publish volcanically, making it hard to spot diamonds in the lava. This is no more than an assay of their interesting ash-slopes. *Soma| Sema* (2011): David Toms orchestrates language under pressure, splices it with images, refracted and found texts. Dazzling. *oh-zones* (2012): Elizabeth-Jane Burnett. Hugely successful experiment in finding forms of embodiment in environments and language. "Whords", she writes, "are words experienced as chords". Affected, but she pulls it off by not being solemn or pseudo-ideological. *the liberation of [placeholder]* (2012): Dylan Harris mixes striking photographs and images with rants and lyrics. Can be exemplary when at his least clangorous. *Phone in the Roll* (2011): Ira Lightman. Deft, funny leftist political poetry and noisy, clumsy, but breathtakingly fine love poems. Much to be recommended. *Gloss* (2012): Giles Goodland continues his intrepid language experiments, this time a thoroughly enjoyable game of A to Z. Elliptical diction can end up sounding like an old buffer in his cups: "'Dustrust dural carageway', old boy!'"– but, like Burnett, he gets away with Oulipean experiment by being playfully true to it. *The Only Life* (2012): Robert Sheppard presents three short stories about poets and poetry. Sheppard has been reading Borges and has come awake to the poetry of prose. These are unquestionably fully-realised works.

SMITH/DOORSTOP. Exceptional record for spotting and nurturing talent. The Poetry Business made marginal poetry central (the new margins are now occupied by the colourful tents of Nine Arches, Penned in the Margins and Pighog Press). When it began in 1986, their pamphlet competition was unique and quietly revolutionary. The writers here are winners from last year's competition judged by Carol Ann Duffy. *Confusion Species* (2012): Suzannah Evans startles and surprises through imagery; her flatness of tone allows defamiliarisation to resonate, e.g. on bitterns:

> The bassoon is recovering
> from a drop in numbers in the '90s
> and is now on the red list.
> It inhabits reedbeds and its boom
> can be heard for miles on still nights.   'Catalogue d'Oiseaux'

That so-easy thing (2012): governing dynamics of Rosie Shepperd's poetry are sensual intelligence and formal erudition. Shepperd's long lines are fearlessly balanced. She builds apparently impossible bridges of register and tone yet still sounds like she were speaking from across the room. Her mind moves ornately yet her poetry is comic, clear and cool – all in their best senses of those words. *Breathing Through Our Bones* (2012): Julie Mellor's title poem blends geology, archaeology and morphology to precise, powerful effect. Many fine poems here yet Mellor could go a good deal further if she allowed her diction to be less straitened by contemporary expectation and literary influence: she needs to let her language fly and fail, then soar. *If We Could Speak Like Wolves* (2012): Kim Moore is the most compelling poet under review because she is least afraid of the dark sounds speaking through her. She welcomes and invokes duende: the unworldly and worldly occupy the same verbal space. Her poetry is always out of the ordinary yet unshowy despite (or because of) her expert and subtle handling of line and form. The result: a balanced arrangement of wild gift and mindful shaping (even a poem about *Watership Down* possesses duende). Moore is also the poet most likely to communicate to people who do not read poetry – yet her work is in no way simple or charming. Much promise yielded, much beckoning for the future.

Finale? Pamphlets are a living form. Seismic energy and imagination compressed into miniature cultural exhalations. Pamphlets are also a literary form, as are reviews.

David Morley's next collection *The Gypsy and the Poet* is due from Carcanet in 2013.

☙

CONTRIBUTORS

Dannie Abse's new volume of poems, *Speak Old Parrot*, will be published by Hutchinson in 2013. **Amy Acre** writes and performs poetry for publication and for spoken-word events. **Graham Allison** is currently completing an MA in Creative Writing at Bath Spa University. **Mona Arshi** lives in London and is currently working towards a first collection. **Tiffany Atkinson** is author of two poetry collections, *Kink and Particle* (Seren, 2006) and *Catulla et al* (Bloodaxe, 2011). **Angelina Ayers** is writer in residence at Bank Street Arts and is studying for an MA Writing at Sheffield Hallam University. **Miles Burrows** works as a locum GP in Cambridge and has published a collection with Cape. **Gerry Cambridge**'s latest book of poems is *Notes for Lighting a Fire* (Happen*Stance* Press, 2012). **C.J. ("Jonty") Driver** has two new books coming out in 2013: *Citizen of Elsewhere*, a pamphlet of poems (Happen*Stance* Press), and *My Brother & I*, a short biography. **Andrew Elliott**'s collection *Lung Soup* was published in 2009. **Carrie Etter** has published two collections, *The Tethers* (Seren, 2009), winner of the London New Poetry Award, and *Divining for Starters* (Shearsman, 2011). **Naomi Foyle** is the daughter of British-Canadian writer Brenda Riches, and the author of two poetry collections from Waterloo Press. **Alice Fulton** received a 2011 Award in Literature from the American Academy of Arts and Letters. **Robin Fulton Macpherson** is a Scottish poet and translator (of Harry Martinson and Tomas TranstRömer among others) who has lived for many years in Norway. **John Gohorry**'s full sequence of *The Age of Saturn* is due to be published by Shoestring Press in 2013. **Michael Hofmann** teaches in Florida and translates from the German; his *New and Selected Poems* appeared in 2008. **Sarah Howe** won an Eric Gregory Award in 2010; she teaches English at Cambridge. **August Kleinzahler** lives in San Francisco and is the author of eleven books of poetry; *The Hotel Oneira* is due from Farrar, Straus & Giroux next year. **Judy Kravis** lives in Ireland; 'His Heroic Youth' will appear in *Flashes and Floaters* (Road Books, 2012). **Hannah Lowe**'s collection *Chick* will be published in 2013 by Bloodaxe. **Karen McCarthy Woolf** is currently Writer in Residence at The November Project, a tidal energy initiative based in the middle of the River Thames. **James McGonigal** is the biographer of Edwin Morgan, and his pamphlet *Cloud Pibroch* (Mariscat Press) won the 2011 Michael Marks Award. **Edward Mackay** was shortlisted for the inaugural Picador Poetry Prize (2011); his debut pamphlet will be published by Salt this autumn. **Patrick Mackie**'s *Excerpts From The Memoirs Of A Fool* was published by Carcanet in 2001. **Hilary Menos**'s *Berg* (Seren, 2009) won the Forward Prize for Best First Collection 2010. **Sinéad Morrissey**'s most recent collection, *There Was Fire in Vancouver*, won the *Irish Times* Poetry Award. **Candy Neubert** is the author of two novels (published by Seren). Originally from New York, **Dan O'Brien** is a playwright and poet living in Los Angeles. **Pascale Petit**'s latest collection, *What the Water Gave Me: Poems after Frida Kahlo* (Seren, 2010), was shortlisted for both the TS Eliot prize and Wales Book of the Year. **Julia Reckless**, a MacDowell Fellow, has work being set to music by American composer and Juilliard professor Philip Lasser. **Declan Ryan** is co-editor of the *Days of Roses* anthology series; his poems and reviews have been published in *Poetry London*, *The Rialto* and elsewhere. **Richard Scott** won the *Wasafiri* New Writing Prize 2011 and was selected as a Jerwood/Arvon poetry Mentee. **Rosie Shepperd** is studying for a PhD at Glamorgan; she was a winner in this year's Poetry Business Competition. **Penelope Shuttle**'s next publication is *UNSENT: New and Selected Poems 1980–2013* (Bloodaxe, 2012). **Julian Stannard**'s latest book is *The Parrots of Villa Gruber Discover Lapis Lazuli* (Salmon, 2011). **Robert Stein**'s first collection *The Very End of Air* was published by Oversteps Books last year. **Liane Strauss** is an American poet living in London; her collection *Leaving Eden* was published by Salt in 2010. **Fred Voss**'s latest collection is *Hammers and Hearts of the Gods* (Bloodaxe). **Rory Waterman**'s first collection will be *Tonight the Summer's Over* (Carcanet, 2013); he edits the poetry and arts magazine *New Walk*. **David Wheatley**'s latest book is *Flowering Skullcap* (Wurm Press). **Ben Wilkinson** is working on a new pamphlet, provisionally titled *Last Hope: poems after Paul Verlaine*. **John Hartley Williams**'s most recent publication is *Assault on the Clouds* (Shoestring Press).

Allison McVety photo: Derek Cooper. Jackie Kay photo: Mary McCartney

NATIONAL POETRY COMPETITION WINNERS 2011 & JACKIE KAY AT CHELTENHAM LITERATURE FESTIVAL

Listen to the poems that won the National Poetry Competition and be transported from Scott's Antarctic all the way to Kashmir, via Virginia Woolf's lighthouse. Readings from prizewinners **Allison McVety**, **Samantha Wynne-Rhydderch** and **Zaffar Kunial**, with judge **Jackie Kay**. An event organised in partnership with the Poetry Society.

Wednesday 10 October, 2pm
At venue L171, IMPERIAL SQUARE
Cheltenham, Glos.

Tickets £6
Box office: 0844 880 8094
Book at cheltenhamfestivals.com/ literature

 THE POETRY SOCIETY

 www.poetrysociety.org.uk

Discover a world of beautiful illustrated editions with The Folio Society

Since 1947, The Folio Society has become one of England's most creative publishing houses. In our 65-year history, we have published an astonishing range of works; from *Moby-Dick* to *The Wonderful Wizard of Oz*, and from the *Bible* to *The Hitchhiker's Guide to the Galaxy*. Our current list includes nearly 400 works of fiction, biography, history, science, children's literature, poetry, philosophy, travel and more.

Books that are beautiful inside and out

Our bindings are crafted in buckram, cotton, silk or leather, and blocked with beautiful designs. We commission new illustrations from artists of the calibre of Quentin Blake, Charles van Sandwyk and Tom Phillips RA. And our editions feature specially commissioned introductions by leading writers such as Umberto Eco for Jacques le Goff's *Medieval Civilisation* and Michael Cunningham, Pulitzer Prize-winning author of *The Hours*, for *Mrs Dalloway*.

There are hundreds of beautifully bound and illustrated Folio editions to discover on our website including the *Selected Poems & Prose* of Gerard Manley Hopkins, the *Selected Poems of Robert Frost* plus *A Folio Anthology of Poetry* and *The Crimson Fairy Book,* both of which are introduced by Poet Laureate Carol Ann Duffy. Visit us now, and you're entitled to FREE delivery of your order.

Binding design *The Selected Poems & Prose* of Gerard Manley Hopkins

Head and tail bands   Exquisite typographic design

Go to www.foliosociety.com/tps

Illustration by Grahame Baker-Smith from Carlo Collodi's *Pinocchio*